SIZA MALAGAMBA
Before After

To my sons, Joana and Álvaro, and to my grandchildren, Henrique and Mariana
To my parents and to Sabine

SIZA MALAGAMBA
Before After

Álvaro Siza
Duccio Malagamba

FOREWORD

The extremes of a building process...

This book originated from the wish to deepen and distill a collaboration that has been developing without interruption since 1993. During this time, Duccio Malagamba has travelled the world to record the fascinating works that Álvaro Siza has disseminated across the planet.

Whenever possible, Malagamba took care to portray each project when it was completely finished, furnished and occupied, in a sense concluding the work that began years earlier by the wise hand of Siza, with subtle pen strokes entrusted to hardback notebooks, loose sheets of paper, envelopes or paper napkins.

It is astonishing how Siza's sketches are able to summarize and anticipate the qualities that may later be contemplated in his built work. The desire to emphasize the ability of his lines — so full of poetry and elegance — to encapsulate the complexity of an entire project is one of the two circumstances that led to the realization of this book, a book that, in order to demonstrate the sketches' almost magical clairvoyance, dares to omit the complexity of design and construction. The abrupt leap from the moment of conception to the conclusive realization, from before to after, is intended to stress the extraordinary richness of the architect's drawings, while Malagamba's rigorous yet delicate images testify to the results.

The other reason that fuelled the existence of this book, a motivation that has sustained Malagamba's unwavering will that one day the work should finally come to light, is much more prosaic: the search for an excuse to be able to spend time with Siza. The desire to find a project in which architect and photographer were involved led Malagamba to devise not a book *about* Siza but one made *with* Siza.

Thanks to the architect's generosity with his time, this is not just another book to add to the many titles dedicated to his work. This is a book that, despite having its origin in an impulse by Malagamba, has been conceived, revised, enriched and modified by both men. The selection of the projects, the compilation of the drawings and the feature texts reflect the architect's own selections, and his reflections have also guided the design of the book and the curation of photographs.

In short, this is a book of singular characteristics. More than this, however, it is a dream achieved for Malagamba, who succeeded in sharing it with the master he so admires.

CONTENTS

INTERIOR—EXTERIOR:
A SINGLE DESIGN

Álvaro Siza

DM: I only took pictures of the exteriors. The interior was not presentable. It looked like a funeral home.

AS: I know, Duccio. Now, it's like this: take the pictures the day *before* the conclusion, [because] soon a brigade of decorators appears. They redo the paint and fill the walls, floor and ceiling with useless objects and very 'modern' furniture. I know this well. They double the intensity of light with spotlights of various colours, installing more smoke detectors and surveillance cameras. They settle in, become ensconced.

Few people consider that interior and exterior are the same thing. In some private homes, the family adapts itself and adapts the house, arguing at length. Incomprehensible contradictions may arise, but there is the value of authenticity, of taking over space with a story behind it, short though that might be, to begin with.

But this happens rarely. Any family with some money will delegate to decorators (interior designers, to put it more elegantly). Soon, some claim the architect is egocentric, a narcissist, does not understand today's reality, has no capacity for dialogue, is not open-minded. Or, quite often, that this is elitist architecture. That is the definitive argument of those who do not care about or who disregard architecture, the essence of its social function: beauty, imperceptible functional effectiveness.

Duccio Malagamba has been photographing my work for years, and that by others, sometimes also the interiors. And when he cannot photograph inside, I can imagine his impatience when, peeking through an open window, he sees a veil of falsehood.

Like the architect, the photographer learns to see with the fresh eyes of a child who has not learned. There are parallel paths for both and for others, especially those who build their own houses, or houses for all, moved by open-eyed dreams.

DM: I only took pictures of the exteriors.

AS: I know, Duccio. Sometimes, you fix what is then destroyed.

006 Preliminary sketch of the Family House in Sintra, Portugal.

WHITE MASTERPIECES
Duccio Malagamba

I fell in love with the architecture of Álvaro Siza once and forever on a sunny afternoon in 1984. My girlfriend and I had decided that year to spend our summer holiday travelling to Portugal with the car that my parents generously lent me. We entered Portugal from the north after driving along the Cantabrian coast, and on reaching Porto — exhausted because of the deplorable road conditions — we stopped at a ramshackle seafront on the outskirts of the city.

Without searching for it — being a third-year architecture student, my information was quite poor, and I was just looking for the Boa Nova restaurant — I found the most beautiful swimming pool I have ever seen in my life. Filled with happy children and blurred by the ocean's waves, the pools at Leça da Palmeira seemed to me a sublime song to Architecture with a capital A — something capable of making Nature homely, even of improving it.

Still, today, when I remember the emotion that simple but brilliant intervention provoked in me, I get the shivers. For an aspiring architect, these pools represented a stunning exemplar and an incredible challenge. Could anyone be more effective with fewer resources? Was it possible to bend a context to human interests with more delicacy? Should I spend my life trying to follow that masterly blazed trail, or was it wiser to give up at the very beginning?

Questions of that kind were probably hovering in my subconscious when, after a few years of working as an architect, I decided to devote myself instead to architectural photography. Needless to say, my interest in Siza's work never disappeared, and I began to portray his buildings regularly. Since the early 1990s, I have done my best to freeze the wide range of sensations I experienced while spending days in buildings he designed, and I would consider myself satisfied if I were able to transmit a quantum of the solace I tasted there.

Meeting Álvaro Siza was another highlight of my life, and since then, I have become fascinated not only by his work but also by his extraordinary personality and courtesy. In fact, the idea for this book arose as an excuse to work closely with him on a common project. It is, of course, bold to show my photographs face to face with his incomparable sketches — masterpieces representing masterpieces — but, as is well known, you do stupid things when in love.

008 Ceilings in the entrance area of
the Galician Centre of Contemporary Art,
Santiago de Compostela, Spain.

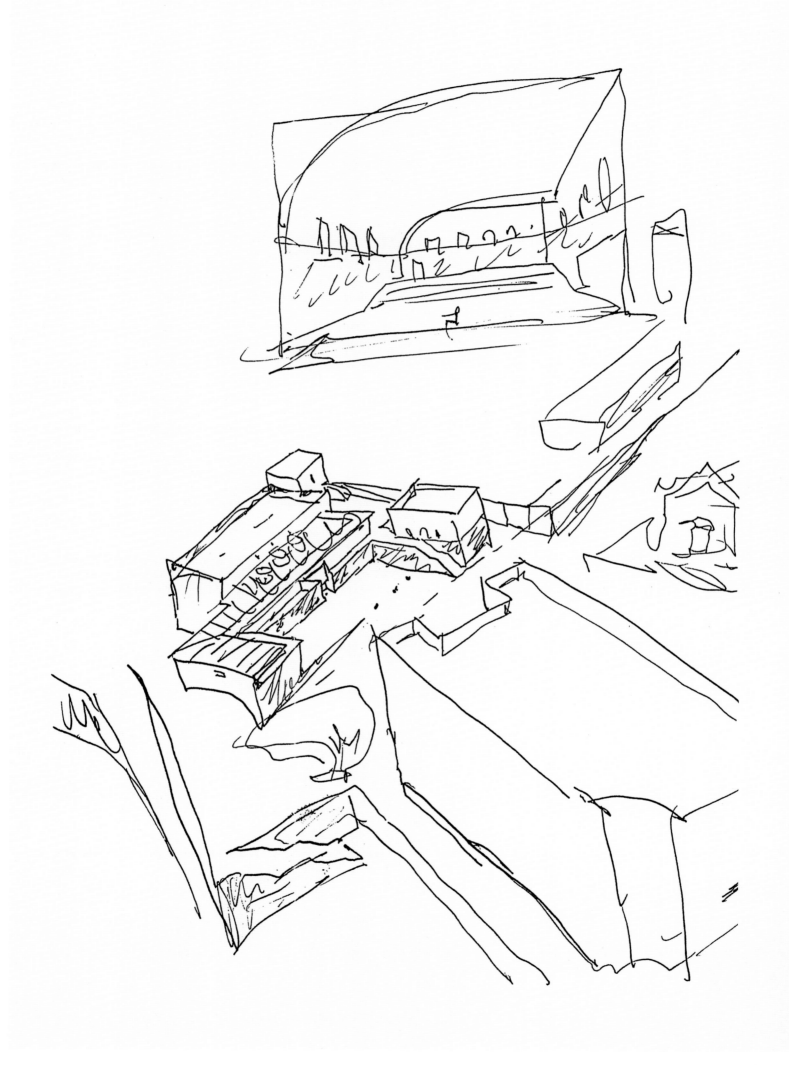

SANTA MARIA CHURCH
AND PARISH CENTRE

Marco de Canaveses, Portugal 1990–2004

The complex is split into two two-storey buildings (consisting of the church and mortuary chapel, auditorium and classrooms) and a three-storey one (the parish residence). The three volumes are articulated with reference to one another and to surrounding buildings in the area, helping to define a central churchyard which is reinforced by the new buildings. This solution gives the imposing church volume a unifying role, with the smaller two volumes more closely aligning with the scale of preexisting buildings on site. Access to the platform on which the complex is set is from the east via a ramp and a wide staircase, and from the west by the existing city streets. The mortuary is accessible directly from the adjoining garden.

The floor plan of the church is rectangular, with a single nave, which has a maximum length of 30 meters (98 ft) and equal width and height (16.5 m/54 ft). The main access and altar are, respectively, at the southwestern and northeastern ends of the longitudinal axis of the nave. The entrance door – 3 meters (10 ft) wide and 10 meters (33 ft) high – is set in a facade 17.5 meters (57 ft) square, made tripartite by the addition of two protruding volumes on either side of the door, each with a floor size of 6 × 5 meters (20 × 16 ft).

The altar space is marked by a narrowing of the nave (owing to the inwardly convex and outwardly concave side wall), by being raised about 0.5 meters (roughly 1½ ft) above the floor of the nave, and by a lateral extension with a ceiling height of 5 meters (16 ft). The altar occupies a central position, surrounded by the lectern and presidential chair, set slightly back towards the nave. Two chairs for the scholars or concelebrants are aligned with the altar, their backs to the side wall. The Tabernacle is on a stone plinth at the threshold of the northwest extension.

The natural lighting of the nave depends on the following architectural elements:
– three openings 3.5 meters wide and 5 meters high (11½ × 16 ft) in the northeastern side wall just below the ceiling, varying in depth because of the curved interior wall;
– a window slot 16 meters long and 0.5 meters high (52½ × 1½ ft), with a sill 1.3 meters (4 ft) above the floor, along the southeastern side wall;
– a light well behind the altar, which also illuminates the mortuary chapel (the light source not being visible); and
– the main entrance, whenever it is open.

The mortuary chapel is beneath the church and level with the ground on the north side of the complex. It is linked directly to the church via stairs and a lift. The main entrance leads in from the garden, mediated by a cloister and its covered wings. From this cloister, it is also possible to have access to the church platform. The height of the mortuary chapel and associated spaces is 6 meters (20 ft).

The baptistery occupies the entire height of one of the set-out volumes next to the main entrance. A vestibule for the side entrance and the stairs to the organ and bells occupy the other. The vestry, office, confessionals and meeting room, as well as the lateral extension of the altar, and the stairs and lift to the mortuary chapel, occupy a rectangular volume of 5 × 25 meters (16 × 82 ft), and 5 meters (16 ft) in height, which is attached to the body of the church.

The auditorium and classrooms are set around two sides of a courtyard, which is open to the north, in front of the church facade and as an extension of the churchyard; the third side is occupied by the parish residence.

010   Study of the parish centre in relation to the church volume, with a first concept for the auditorium.

011

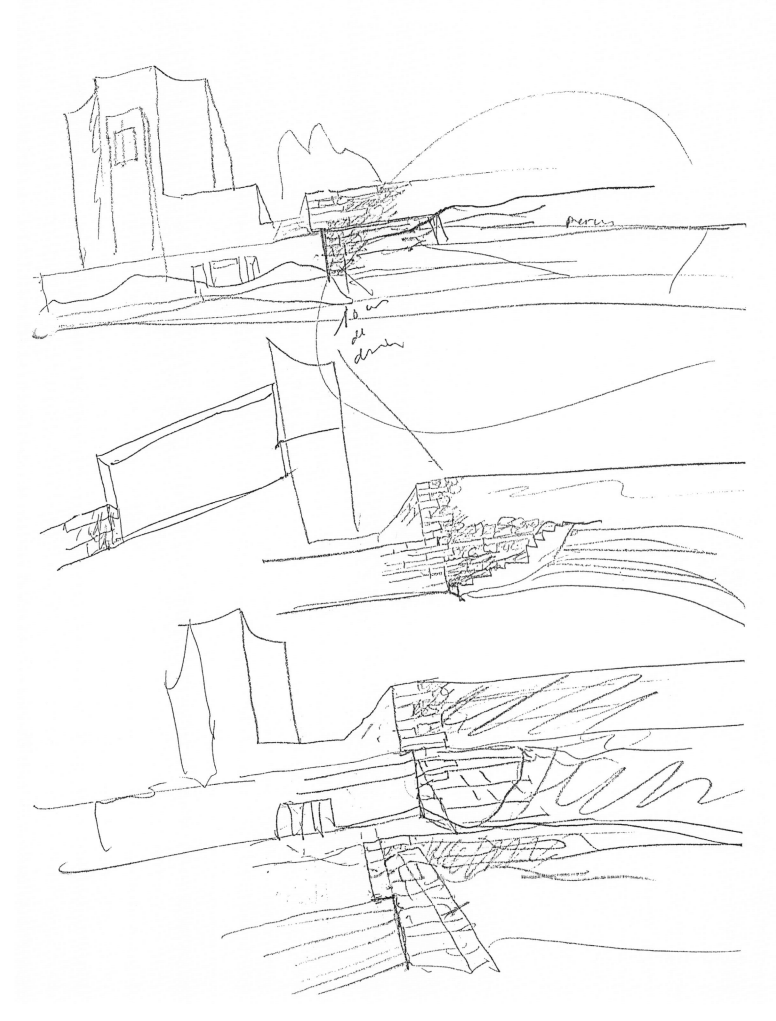

012   Sketch of various solutions for the apse
and rear entrance.
013   The apse seen from the main road which
leads to the town centre.

SANTA MARIA CHURCH AND PARISH CENTRE

415 4/96

014 Sketch of the west elevation with the ancient
chapel in the foreground.
015 West elevation with the protruding sacristy
volume visible.

016 Main entrance facade.
017 Interior view of the entrance and nave
from the altar.

018   Sketch of the nave.
019   The nave, looking from the entrance
towards the altar.

SANTA MARIA CHURCH AND PARISH CENTRE

020 Sketch of the nave showing the curved wall.
021 Ceiling view from the nave.

SANTA MARIA CHURCH AND PARISH CENTRE

022 Baptistery flanking the main entrance.
023 Ceiling of the altar area, with the golden crucifix
in the foreground.

SANTA MARIA CHURCH AND PARISH CENTRE

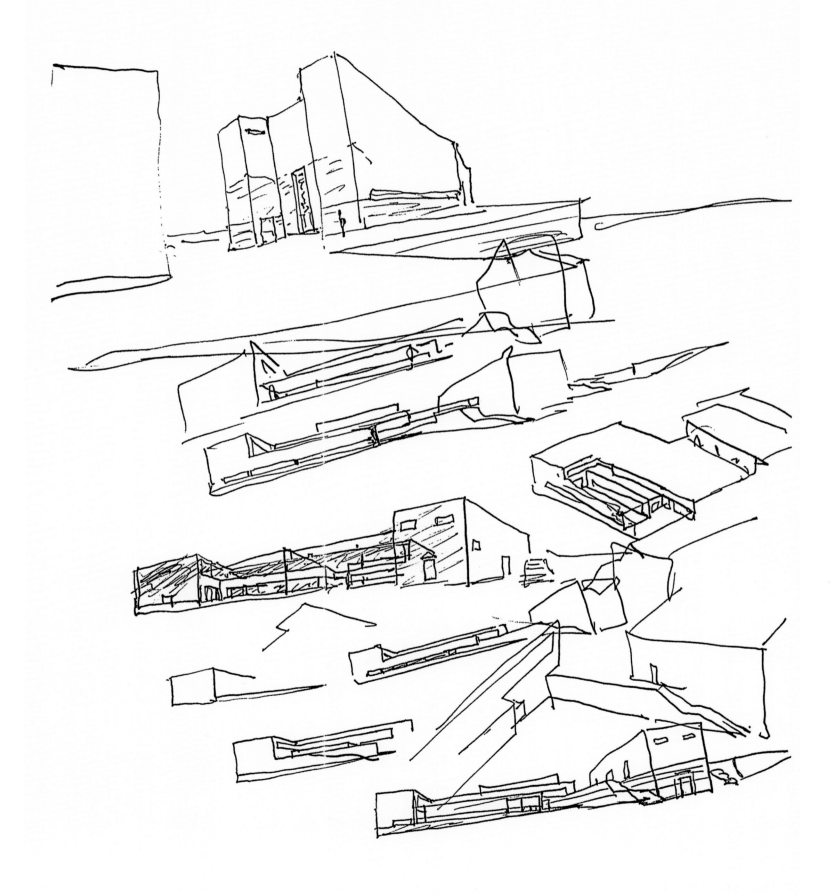

024 Studies of the parish centre.
025 Partial view of the church from the northeast,
with parish centre in the background.

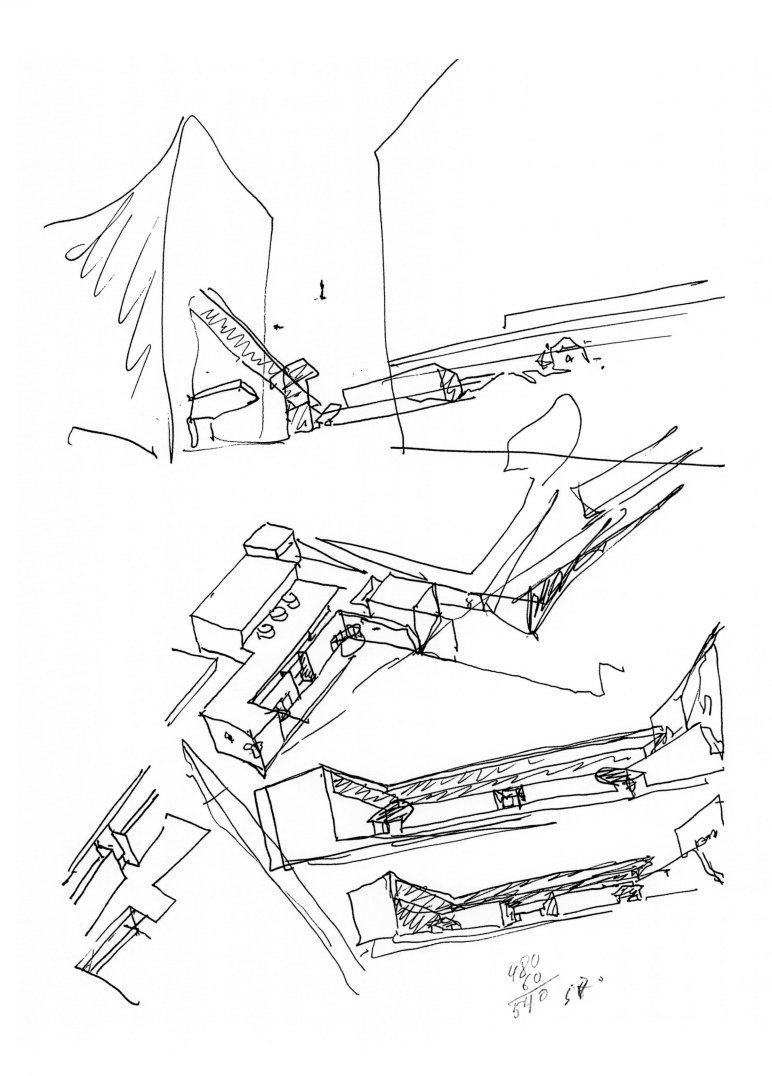

480
60
540 ...

026   Sketches of the parish centre.
027   Top: The parish centre seen from the ancient chapel. Centre: A walkway borders the complex to the southeast. Bottom: The green courtyard of the parish centre.

028 East elevations of parish centre and church.
029 Auditorium of the parish centre.

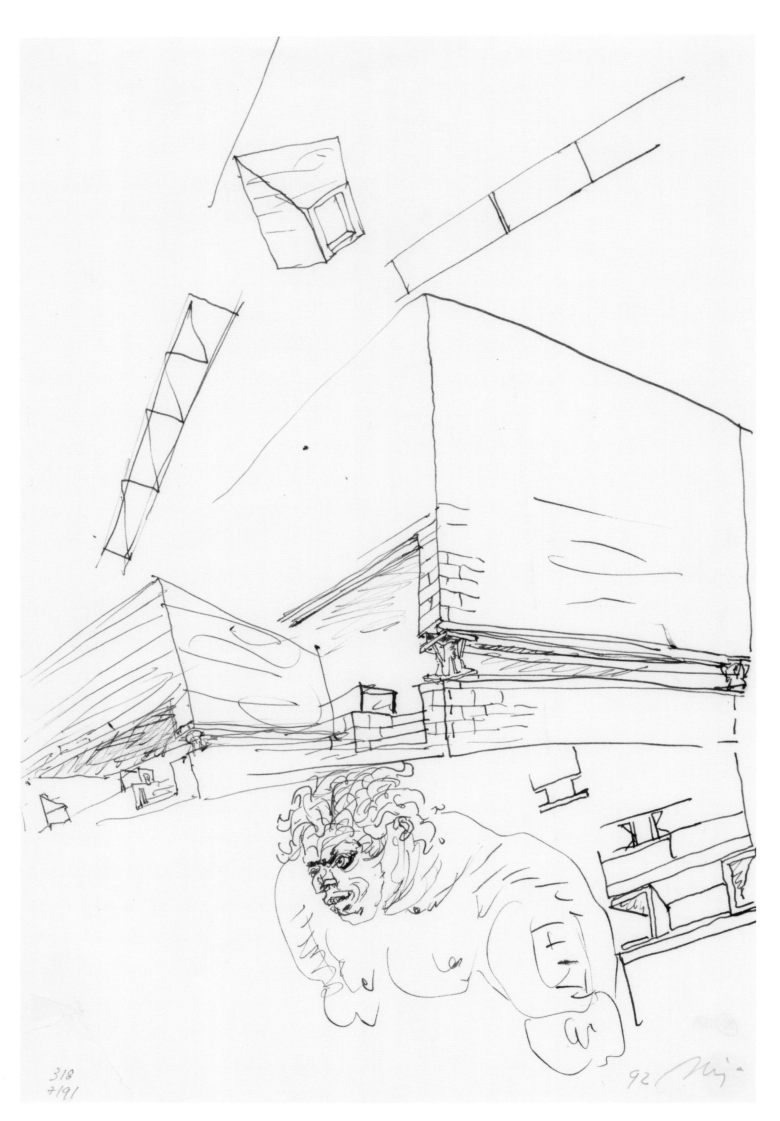

318
7/91

92

GALICIAN CENTRE OF CONTEMPORARY ART

Santiago de Compostela, Spain 1988 —1993

The building of the Galican Centre of Contemporary Art is located within the former orchard of the Convent of San Domingos de Bonaval on Rúa de Ramón del Valle-Inclán, on a succession of terraces between Porta do Camiño and San Domingos. It also allowed for the recovery of the garden east of the Convent of San Roque and the terraces leading to the Convent of San Domingos, with the aim of re-establishing a destroyed pre-existing footprint. The museum fronts the street (which was built in the 1970s), replacing the demolished wall of the convent garden.

The building is characterized by two volumes containing three floors and an accessible terrace, both with an L-shaped floor plan, set roughly on a north—south alignment and converging at the southern extreme. These two bodies determine a triangular intermediate space.

The exhibition areas on the first and second floors are a succession of rooms at different levels and with varying dimensions. The narrow gap between the south-ern extreme of the museum and the front of the convent defines the access to the garden, complemented by the volume of a small, restored structure. This space announces the beginning of the ramps and stairs that connect the building platforms to the park, which is above interlacing terraces at a higher elevation.

030 Studies for the main entrance.

032 Sketches of the overall volume with the
Convent of San Domingos de Bonaval nearby.
033 Overview of the site with the convent
in the background.

275
8/88

034 Plan studies with sketches of the interior spaces.
035 The complex seen from the south.

GALICIAN CENTRE OF CONTEMPORARY ART

036 Detail of the southeast facade.
037 Top: Roof terrace with the convent in the
background. Centre: View of the museum from
the north. Bottom: Southeast facade.

038 Study for the auditorium entrance.
039 Exhibition space.

Adolf Loos: impressão de coisa clara
impressão de luxo, coisa preciosa,
?, reconhecível
continuidade — vezer decorativismo (Charme
Relação com Tessenow ?
sublimação

Livros
consultar
- Loos
- Tessenow
- Charreau
- Tosro
- Corbusier

artesanato
O 1º corbusier

348
7/93

040 Studies for the bookshop and cafeteria area.
041 Top: Auditorium foyer. Centre: Second-floor
space between the administration area and seminar
rooms. Bottom: Cafeteria.

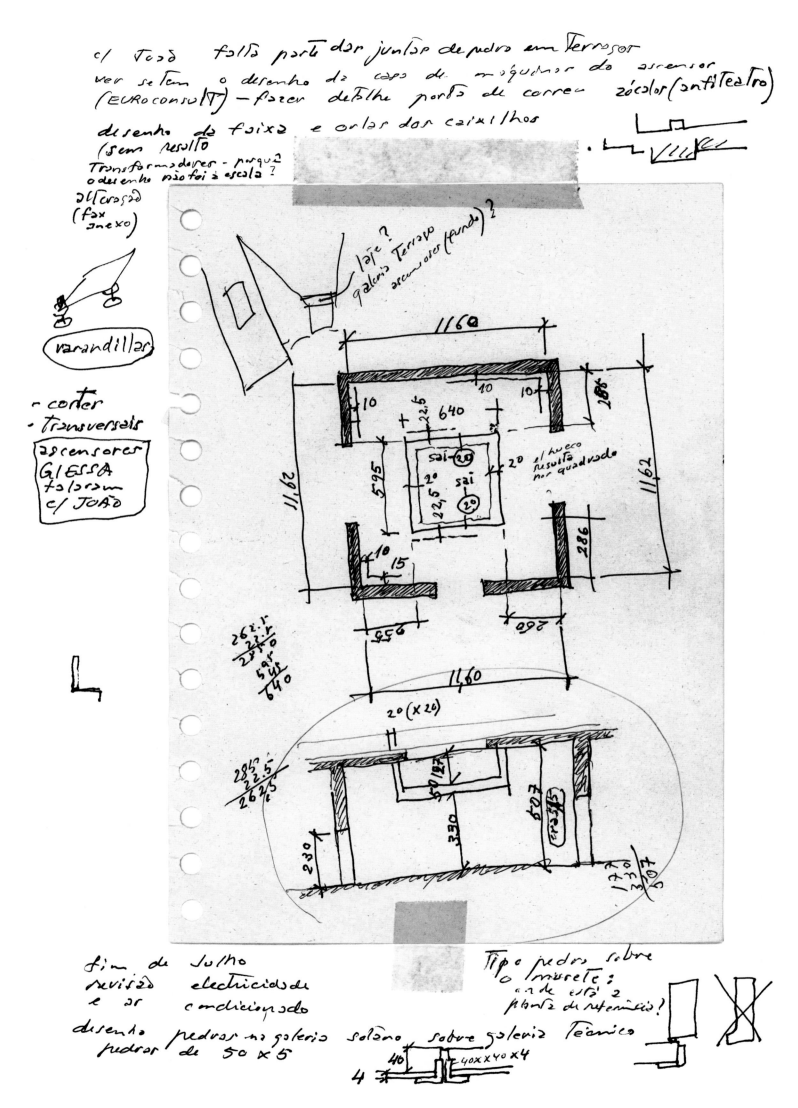

042 Studies for the exhibition galleries.
043 Main staircase leading to the second-floor
exhibition areas.

GALICIAN CENTRE OF CONTEMPORARY ART

318
7/91

044 Sketch of the overhead lighting for the
exhibition galleries.
045 A permanent exhibition gallery overlooking
the temporary exhibition space.

FACULTY OF INFORMATION SCIENCES
Santiago de Compostela, Spain 1993—2000

Housing the Faculty of Information Sciences in the Burgo das Nacións (City of Nations), the 127-meter-long (417-foot-long) building integrates into the existing campus plan. The main body of the building evolves linearly from east to west, respecting the alignment of the philology faculty nearby. Due to the complex topography of the site, this main volume has three floors: a ground floor and two floors above in the western half, and a basement, ground floor and first floor in the rest of the building. Amphitheatre classrooms, accessed by a ramp, lift and stairs, occupy the spaces with the tallest ceilings. The teachers' offices are on the top floor. The lower-height area contains studios for radio and visual arts and audiovisual laboratories.

All of the spaces are arranged along a gallery that faces north. The main lobby is between these two sections of the building, while the gallery also gives access to three volumes inserted perpendicularly, between 7 and 10 meters (23—33 ft) high, which define courtyards opening on to Avenida de Castelao.

The volume in the western end of the gallery contains a 300-seat auditorium, while the remaining two volumes on the eastern side features an audiovisual area along with television and film studios. The library occupies a central position accessible from the two-storey lobby, and its volume defines a broad entrance porch. The stairs, lifts and lavatories are distributed evenly along the main gallery.

046 Isometric sketch of the whole project.

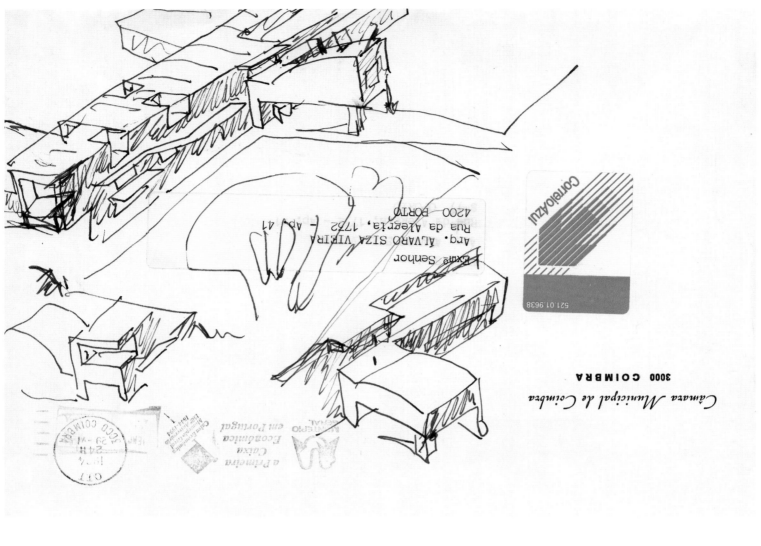

048 Study sketches of the main entrance
and the library volume.
049 The project seen from the southwest.

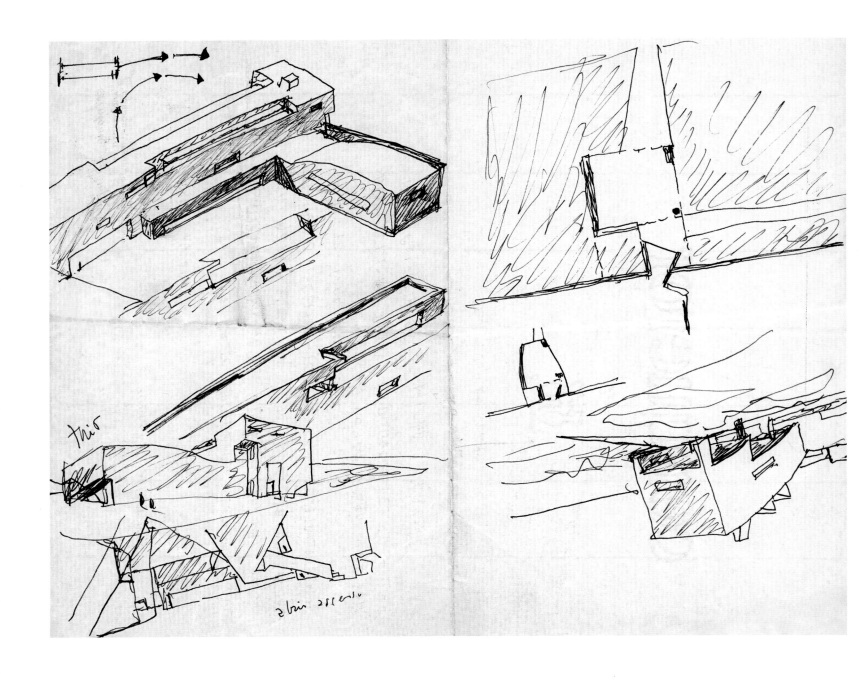

050 Studies for the auditorium, library and main entrance.
051 West elevation, with the auditorium volume
in the foreground.

FACULTY OF INFORMATION SCIENCES

Terreror

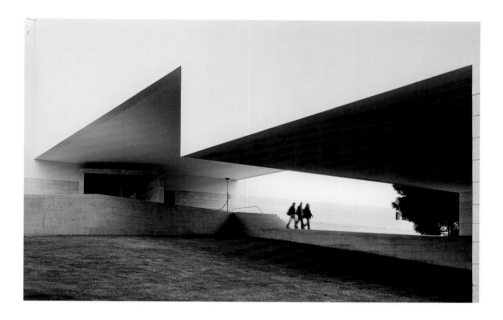

052 Studies for the library and main entrance.
The handwriting reads, 'Everything must be perfect
within the human imperfection, the gods from far
away observe our distractions'.
053 Top: The library volume from the southeast.
Centre: The main entrance underneath the gigantic
canopy of the library volume. Bottom: Opposite
view of the canopy.

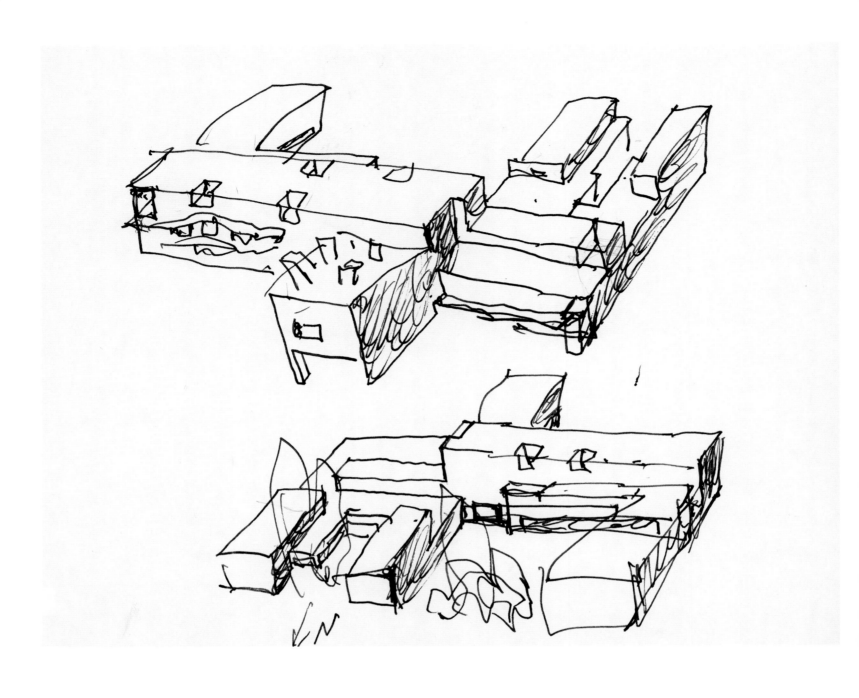

054 Isometric views of the complex from the southeast
(top) and northeast (bottom).
055 The northeastern courtyard is flanked by the blind
walls of the television and film studios.

FACULTY OF INFORMATION SCIENCES

056 Corridor and ramp accessing the classrooms.
057 Main entrance hall.

058 Sketch of the library interior.
059 Library.

SERRALVES MUSEUM OF CONTEMPORARY ART

Porto, Portugal 1991–1999

The project for the new Museum of Contemporary Art, on the grounds of the Serralves estate, develops a core of new buildings, autonomous and independent from earlier ones on the site. Key factors influencing the choice of location were the proximity of Avenida do Marechal Gomes da Costa and Rúa Dom João de Castro, ensuring easy public access, and the lack of afforestation, thus avoiding the removal of park trees. The project included the refurbishment of the outdoor spaces around the building and its connection with the estate's historic garden.

Morphologically described, the new building can be seen to develop along a longitudinal axis clearly orientated north–south. All parts of the programme are contained within a single volume, a central body from which project two asymmetrical arms to the south (defining a courtyard) and an L-shaped volume to the north. The latter, in conjunction with the central body, produces another courtyard in the public entrance area. The volume of the building is defined externally by vertical surfaces with a stone basement, maintaining a roof of consistent height and following the variations of the terrain at ground level (the height difference along the entire building is 9 m (30 ft), which corresponds to a slope of 5.3 per cent, descending from north to south).

The main volume encompasses three floors (four in places, through the insertion of a mezzanine). The highest part of the site corresponds with the public entrance to the complex, where access is constrained by a wall, defining a space where paths from the street, underground car park and western garden converge. That is, the various routes available for public access meet at one point, where access to the park is controlled. A covered path leads to the ticket office and from there to a second, large courtyard that allows access to the interior of the museum and the auditorium foyer (via an independent entrance).

The exhibition area is divided into several rooms, all with varying characteristics of scale, proportion, light and space, joined by a broad U-shaped gallery. This circulation space occupies much of the entrance floor and extends into one of the south-facing arms. The doors between the rooms allow the creation of varying exhibition configurations and independent routes for the visitor.

The programme also includes a bookshop, cafe, library and multipurpose rooms, as well as administration offices, facilities for the auditorium and exhibition spaces, and technical areas.

060 Sketch of the access path and courtyard.

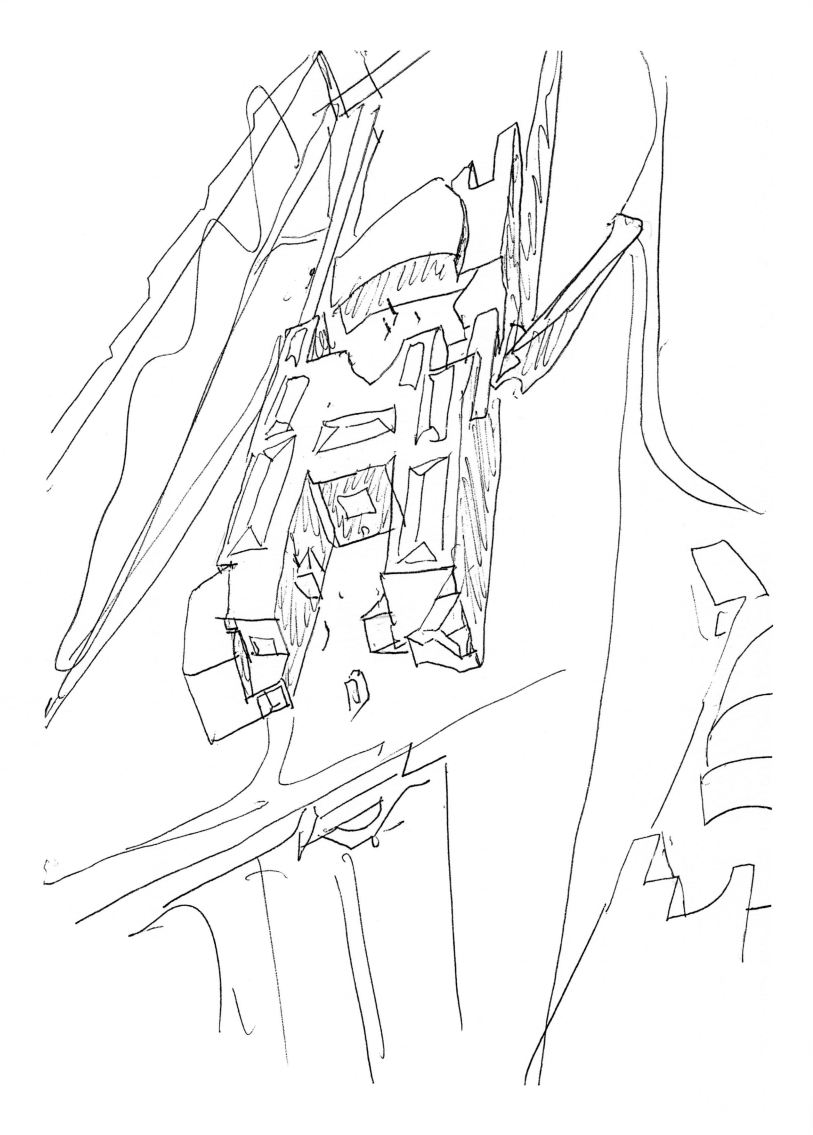

062 Isometric sketch of the whole project.
063 Main access path.

this

064 Studies for the southeastern courtyard.
065 Top: Stairway to the southeastern courtyard.
Centre: East elevation seen from the south.
Bottom: East elevation seen from the north.

SERRALVES MUSEUM OF CONTEMPORARY ART

066 West side of the courtyard in front of the
museum entrance.
067 East side of the courtyard in front of the museum
entrance, showing the access to the gardens.

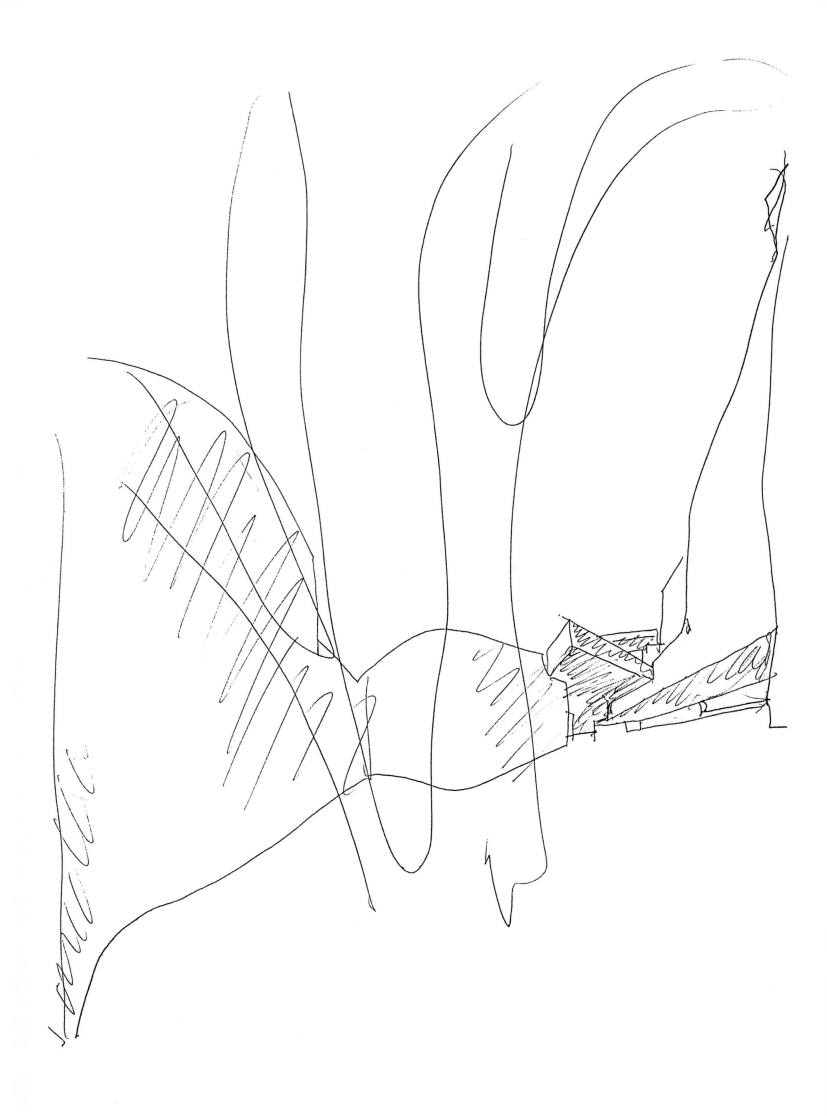

068 Study for the courtyard in front of the main entrance.
069 Detail of the west facade showing the visual
connection with the entrance courtyard.

070   Preliminary sketches of interior and exterior spaces.
071   Exhibition galleries.

072 Studies for the main entrance hall.
073 Main entrance hall.

SERRALVES MUSEUM OF CONTEMPORARY ART

ZAIDA BUILDING AND COURTYARD HOUSE

Granada, Spain 1998—2006

This building, which includes apartments, offices and retail spaces, occupies three previously built-up plots: those of the old Zaida hotel, a recently constructed four-storey building and a house of some architectural value that was developed around two courtyards in accordance with the typology of Granada's ancient urban fabric. Beginning in the late nineteenth century, Plaza del Campillo (the adjoining square) was transformed both architecturally and spatially, causing the traditional urban fabric of buildings and open spaces to disappear as a result. After the channelling of the Darro River in 1884, however, the plaza became increasingly important, and it now dominates the city centre.

The ancient house was maintained, along with its two courtyards. The other buildings were demolished to allow the construction of a new six-storey volume. The approximate height of the surrounding buildings act as a culmination of the block and a new front to the square. The broken shape of the west facade follows the ancient trace of the river. From the third floor of the facade overlooking Carrera de la Virgen, the building opens in a U shape to allow a better view of the Alhambra.

076 Sketch of the building in context.
077 The finished building in context, with Plaza del Campillo in the foreground.

078 Early volumetric studies.
079 Axial view of the main facade on Plaza del Campillo,
showing its peculiar, imperfect symmetry.

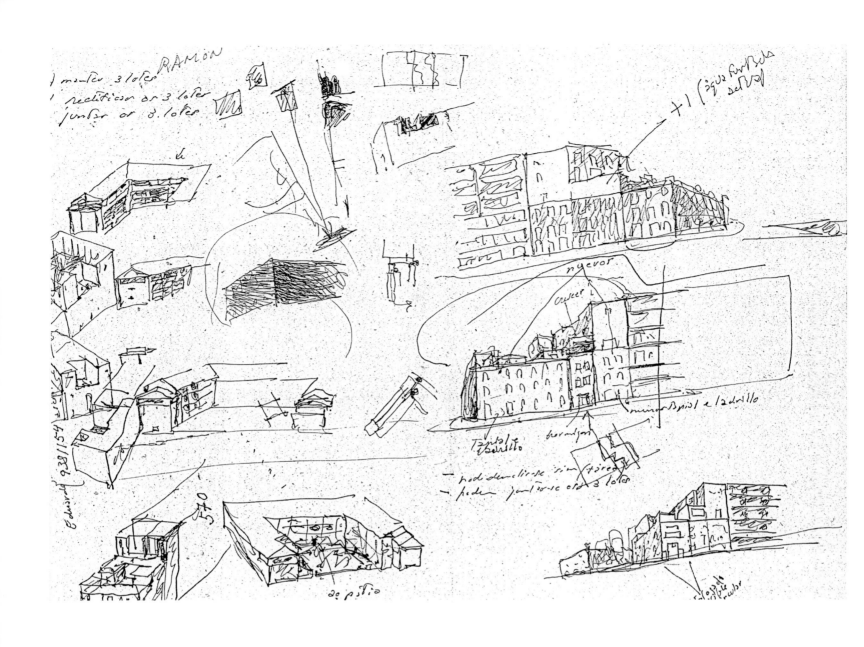

080 Preliminary studies.
081 Partial view of the building from a narrow side street.

ZAIDA BUILDING AND COURTYARD HOUSE

082 Sketch of the lower volume's roof terrace,
overlooking the Alhambra. The note in the bottom
right reads: 'García Lorca in my restaurant in Granada.'
083 Top: The roof terrace with the gardens of the
Generalife in the background. Bottom: The side facade
of the roof terrace.

084 Sketch of the inner courtyard.
085 Inner courtyard, showing the recovered columns
and fountain. The space between the capital of the
column and the volume above it emphasizes the history
of the site, as these columns are no longer structural.

086 Mezzanine exhibition space.
087 Ground floor lobby area of a bank branch located in the complex.

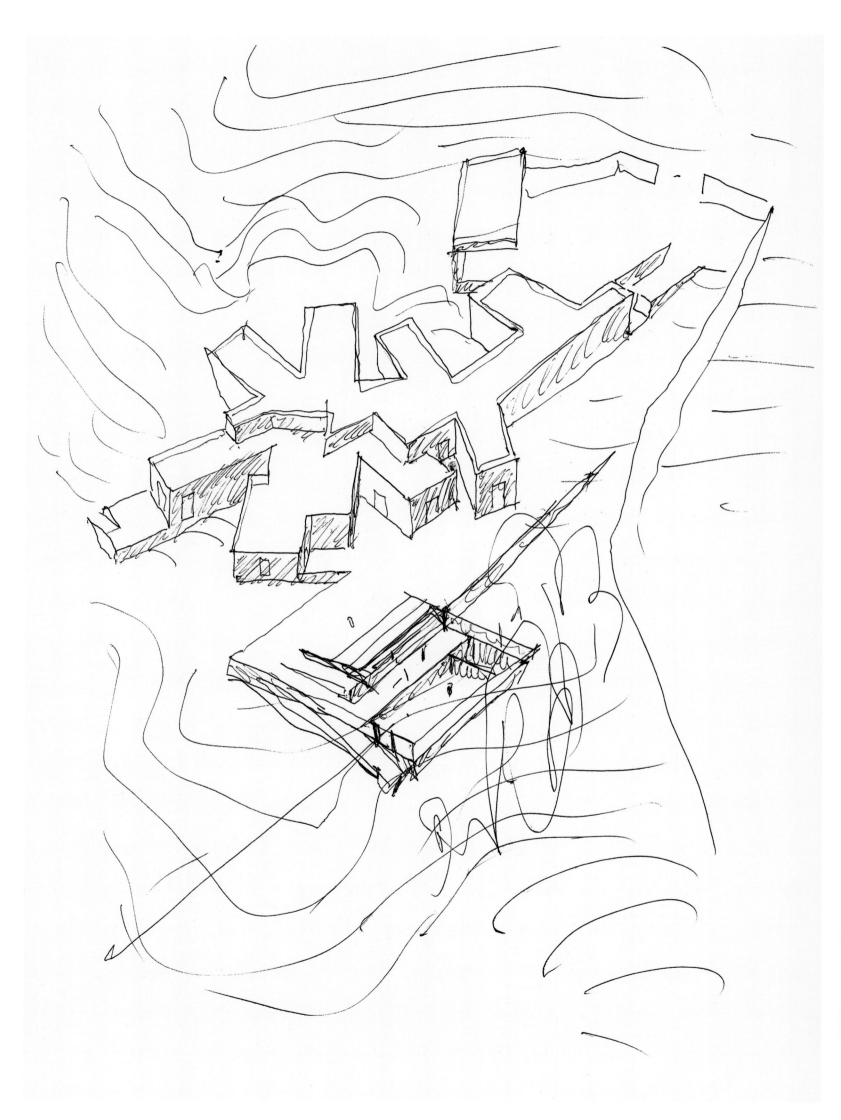

FAMILY HOUSE

Sintra, Portugal 2002–2007

This large (21,680 sq. m/230,000 sq. ft) plot, orientated north-northwest and facing the sea, unravels over a considerable slope. The building is set on a platform on the highest part of the plot, overlooking two magnificent beaches: Praia das Maçãs and Praia Grande.

The programme is contained within semi-independent volumes, arranged along an inner route that constitutes the only common circulation across the house. It leads from an exterior arrival space to the most private core, giving access to the various areas of the programme: five bedrooms, a small office, a large sitting room and a kitchen.

The articulation of the volumes defines irregularly shaped outdoor spaces that create semi-private patios, allowing the creation of openings orientated to all landscape views. Although developed on one floor, the house is organized over four distinct levels, following the terrain. A carport and outdoor pool complete the programme.

088   Isometric sketch of the complex.

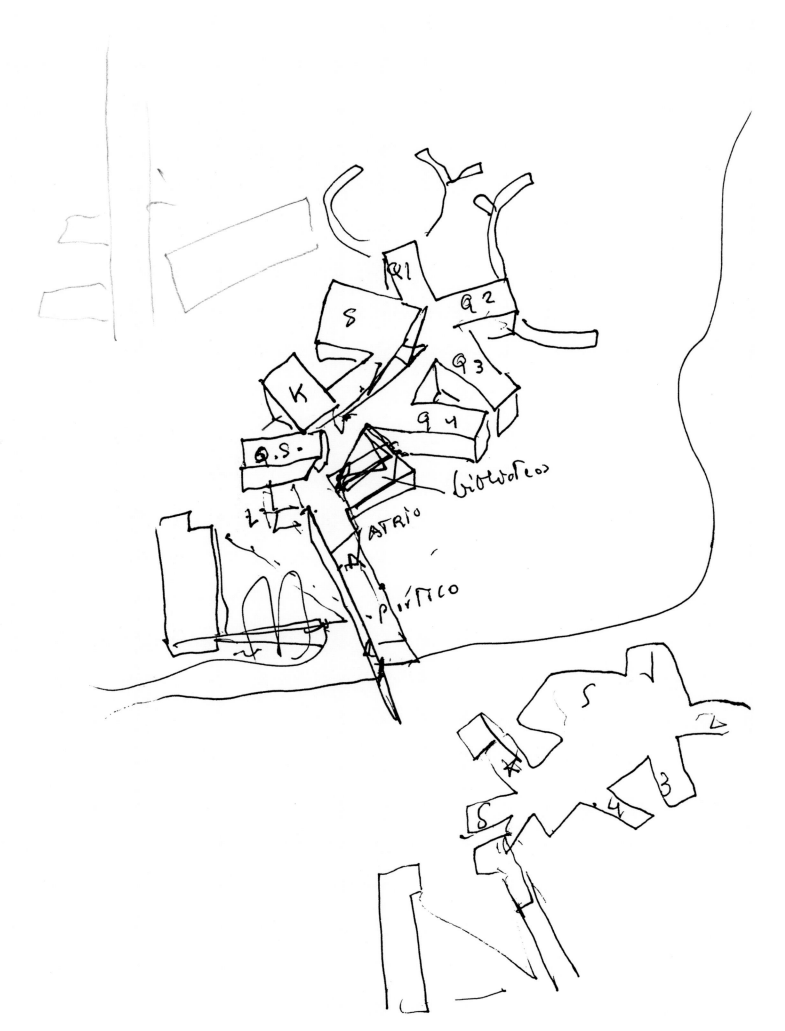

090 Preliminary aggregation schemes.
091 Top: The house at dusk, seen from the swimming–
pool garden. Centre: A green roof with the ocean in
the background. Bottom: Main entrance.

FAMILY HOUSE

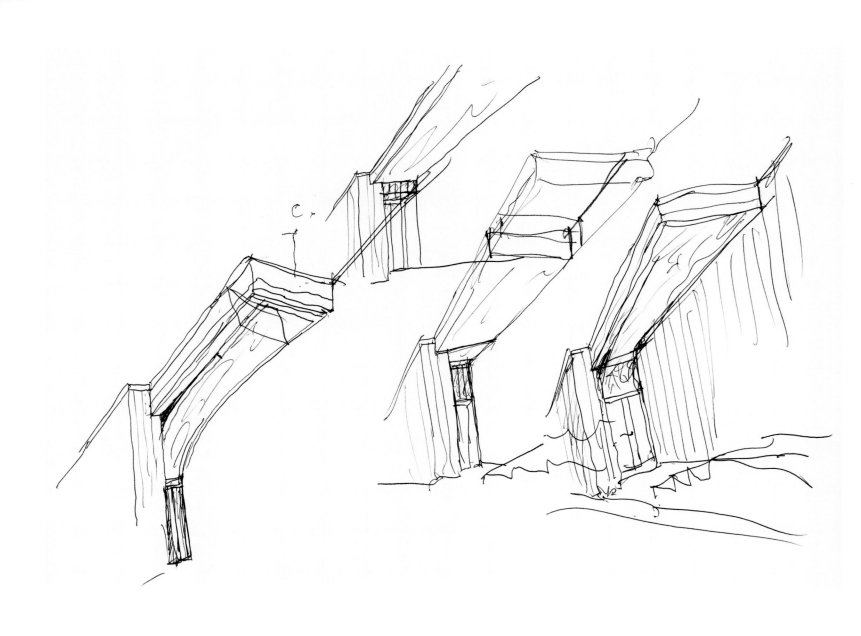

092 Studies for the main entrance.
093 Main entrance side walls.

FAMILY HOUSE

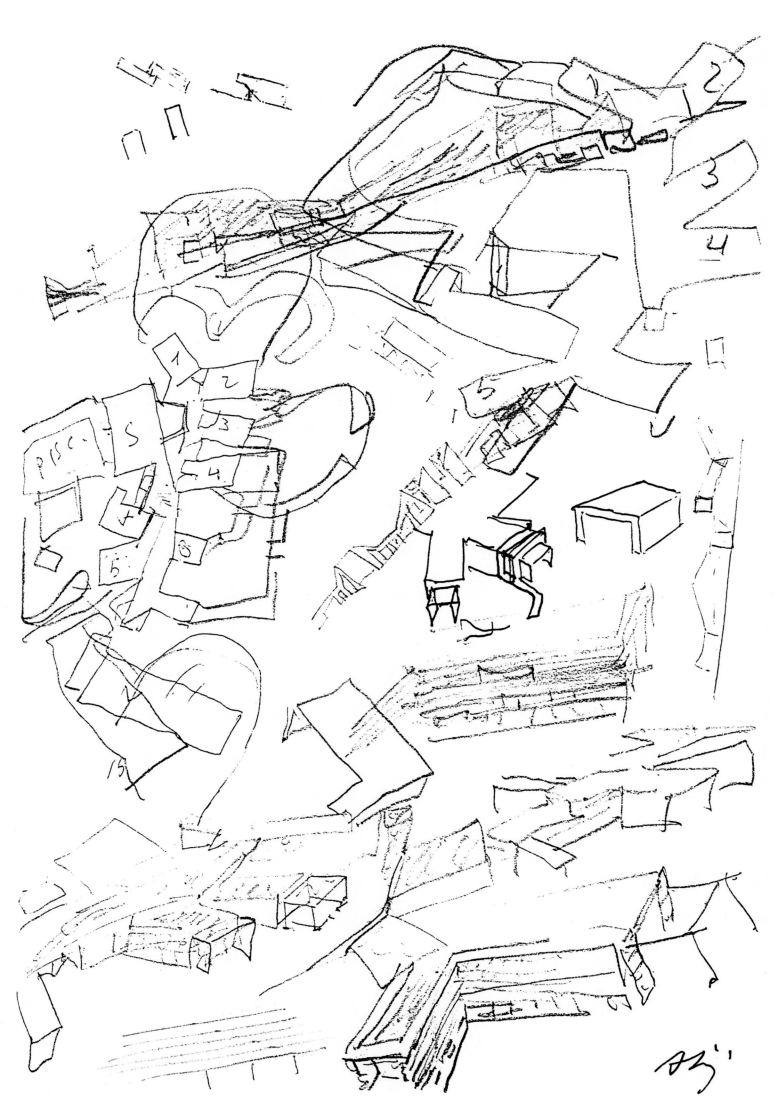

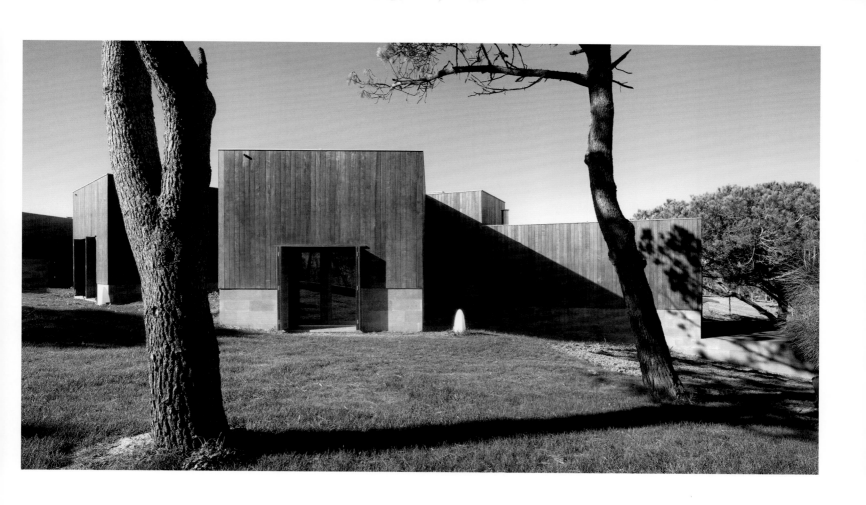

094 Early studies.
095 Exterior view from the east.

FAMILY HOUSE

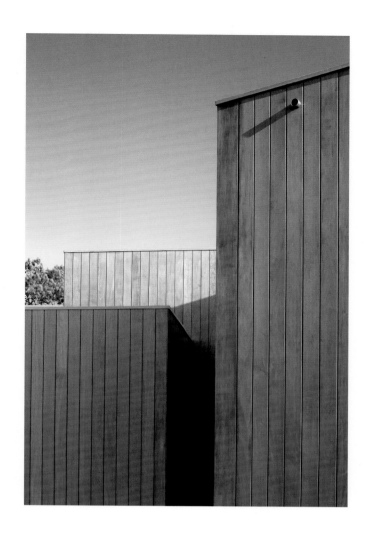

096 Partial view of the backyard.
097 Details of the timber–wrapped volumes.

FAMILY HOUSE

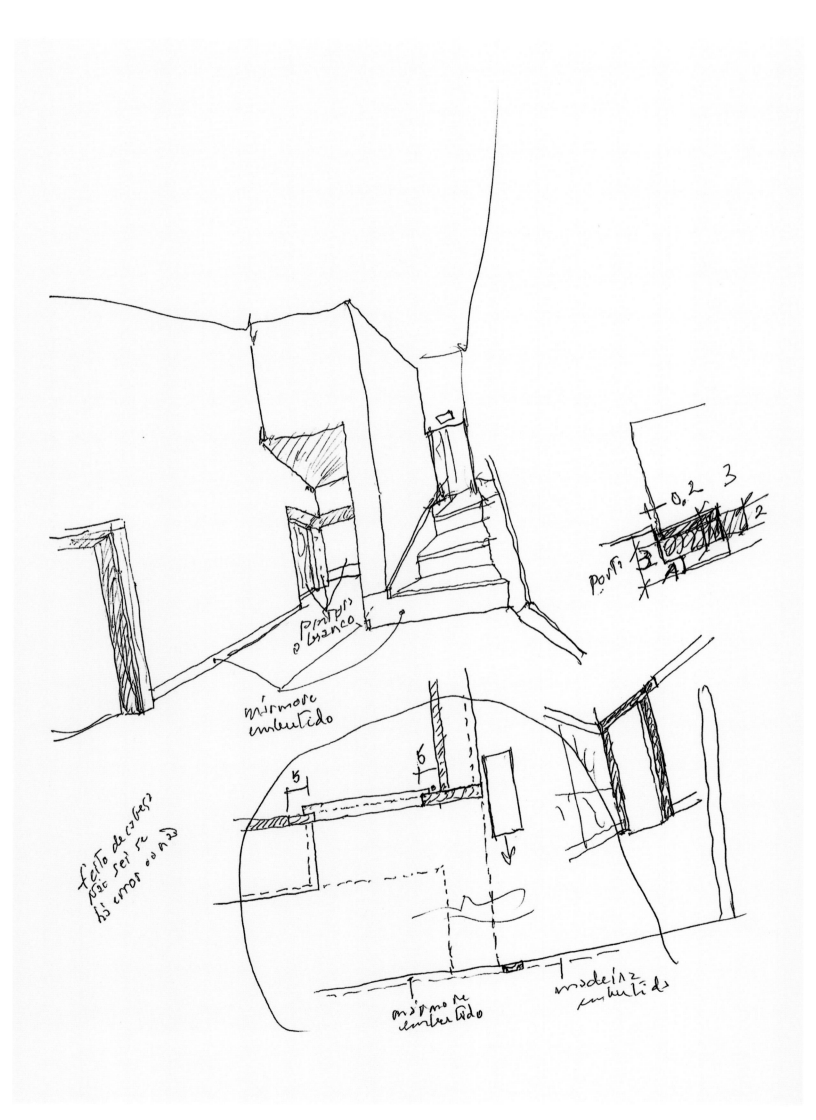

mármore
embutido

pintar
o branco

porta

feito de cabeça
não sei se
há erros 00,23

mármore
embutido

madeira
embutido

098 Sketches of the interior.
099 The main corridor acts as a spine for the entire house.

FAMILY HOUSE

exterior

paredes {reboco s/ pintura (soalho ocre ou rosa)
ou { reboco d/ com incorporada

cobertura zinco ▭▭

caixilharias
madeira pintada

{ou impregnada
escuro
ou teca s/ verniz
(v. Bélgica)

algum painel em azulejo? p/ exemplo garagem, acesso, algum pátio
pavimentos exteriores – guias, degraus etc. em calcáreo
superfícies em betuminoso drenantes s/ juntas
cinza claro

muros suporte reboco igual ao da casa
revestimento piscina paredes azulejo
reboco/fundo cimento branco areado

interior pavimentos tudo em mármore excepto quartos e biblioteca
paredes estucadas
(detalhe tipo) esquadrias madeira à vista portas, rodapés, molduras, armário
semi-aplicada (até 2.10)

① biblioteca estantes em madeira à vista
q. banho soalho mármore até à porta

louça sanitária suspensa branca
torneiras bonitas
pavimentos irradiantes
{ar condicionado? ou vidros com aquecimento – refrigeração?

detalhe silva

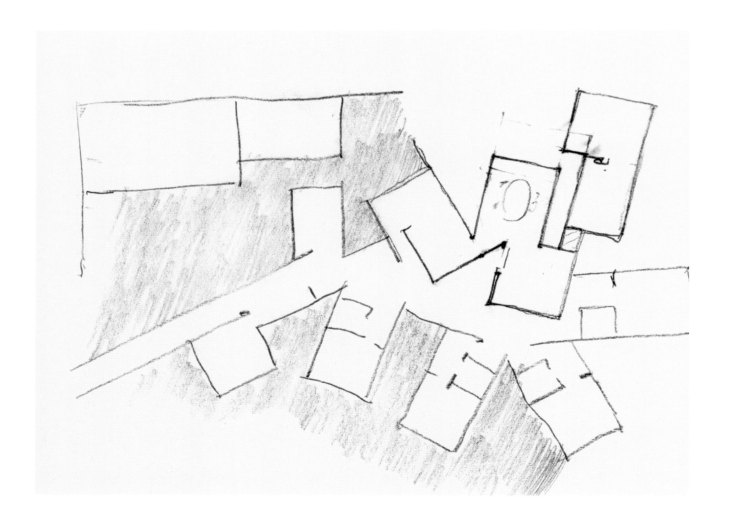

100 Plan and construction specifications.
101 Top: Main corridor, with the entrance door open
in the background. Bottom: The sitting room and dining
room are connected by a sliding door.

FAMILY HOUSE

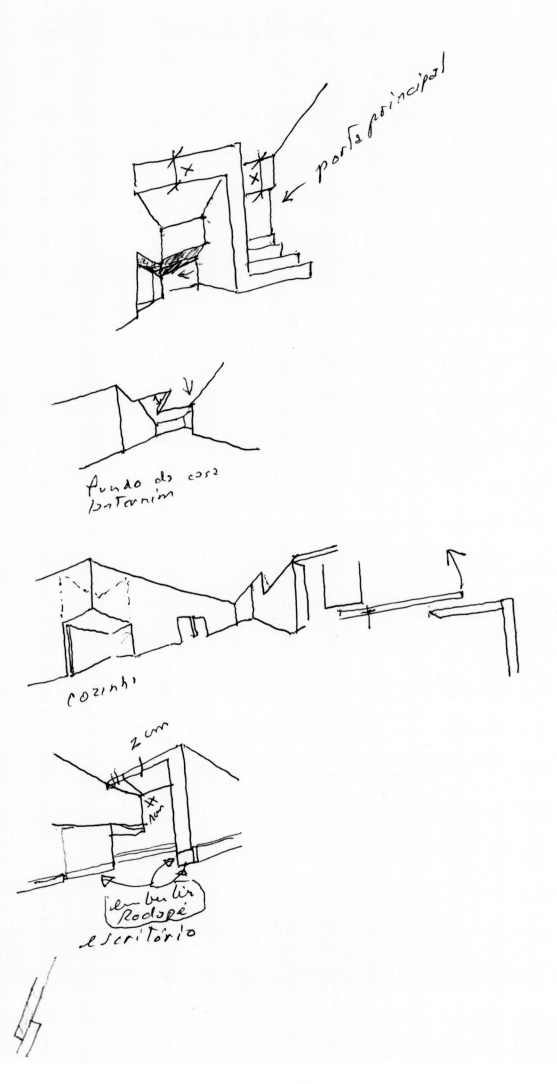

porta principal

fundo da casa
batanim

cozinha

2 cm

embutir
Rodapé

escritório

102 Interior studies.
103 The main corridor culminates in a skylight.

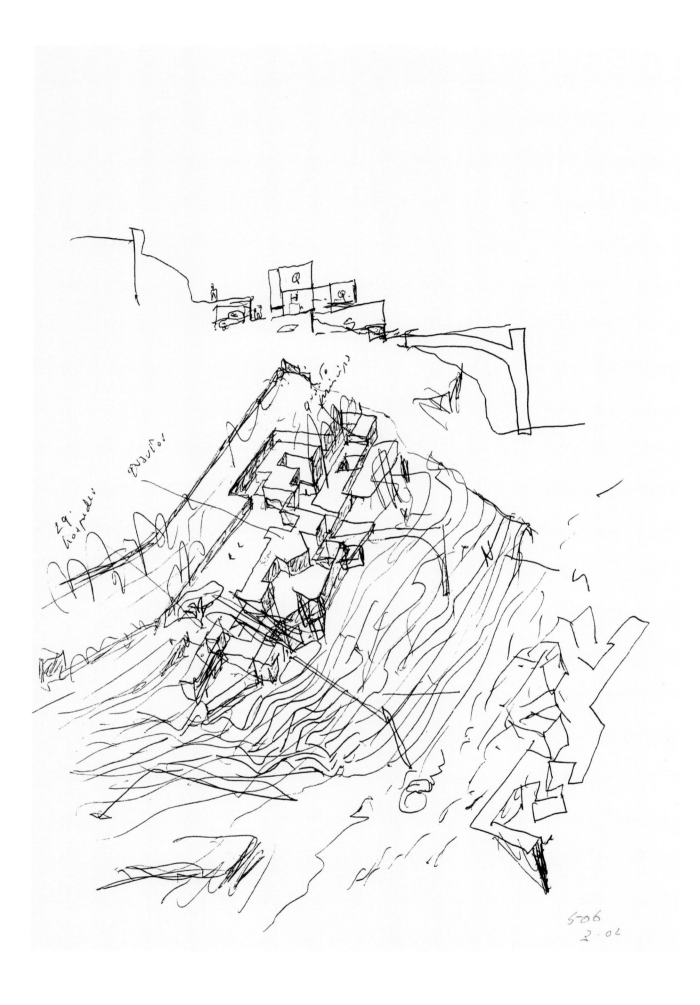

SUMMER HOUSE

Majorca, Spain 2002–2008

Located in Majorca, an island in the Mediterranean Sea, the house sits upon terrain that is characterized by a steep slope. The property is accessed from the north-west, at the highest point of the plot, about 26 meters (85 ft) above sea level, and the house follows a fragmented volumetric composition that extends along the slope.

The building is set 5 meters (16 ft) from the access road, to comply with planning regulations. There is also a separation of 20 meters (66 ft) from the coastline. The solution consists of three two-storey volumes on a platform that is 22 meters (72 ft) above sea level. The private areas of the programme are at the top of each volume, while the common areas (lounges, kitchen, and service spaces) occupy the lower levels. The roof garden emphasizes the house's integration into the landscape.

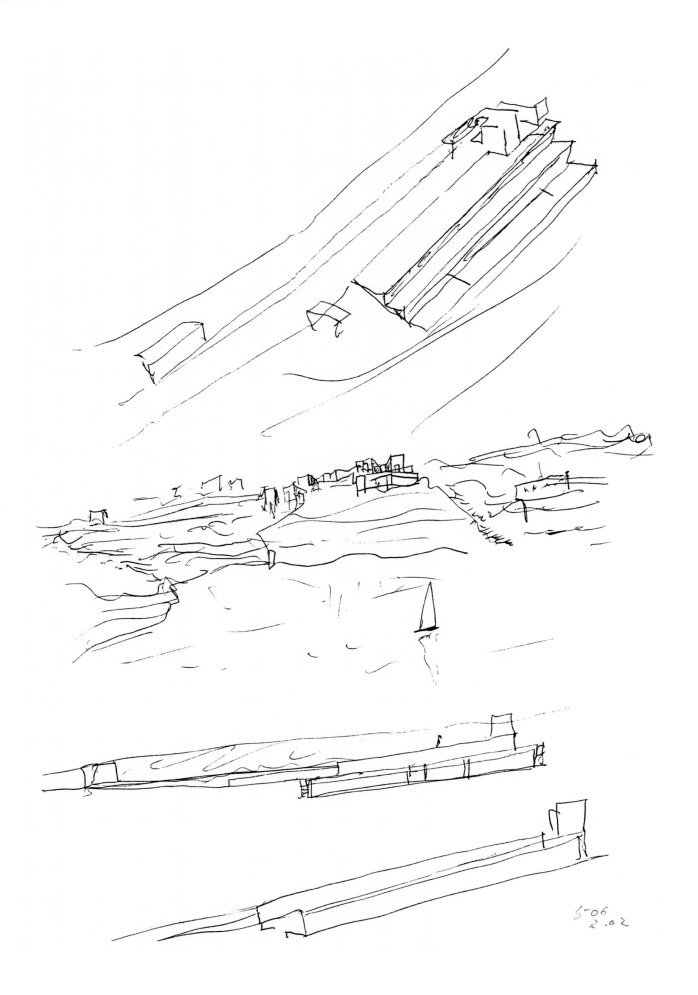

106 Preliminary studies with distant view.
107 Distant view from the small island facing the complex.

108 Schematic study of the overall volume, with sections.
109 The main facade seen from sea level.

SUMMER HOUSE

110   Rear volumes facing the slope.
111   Access path leading to the main entrance.

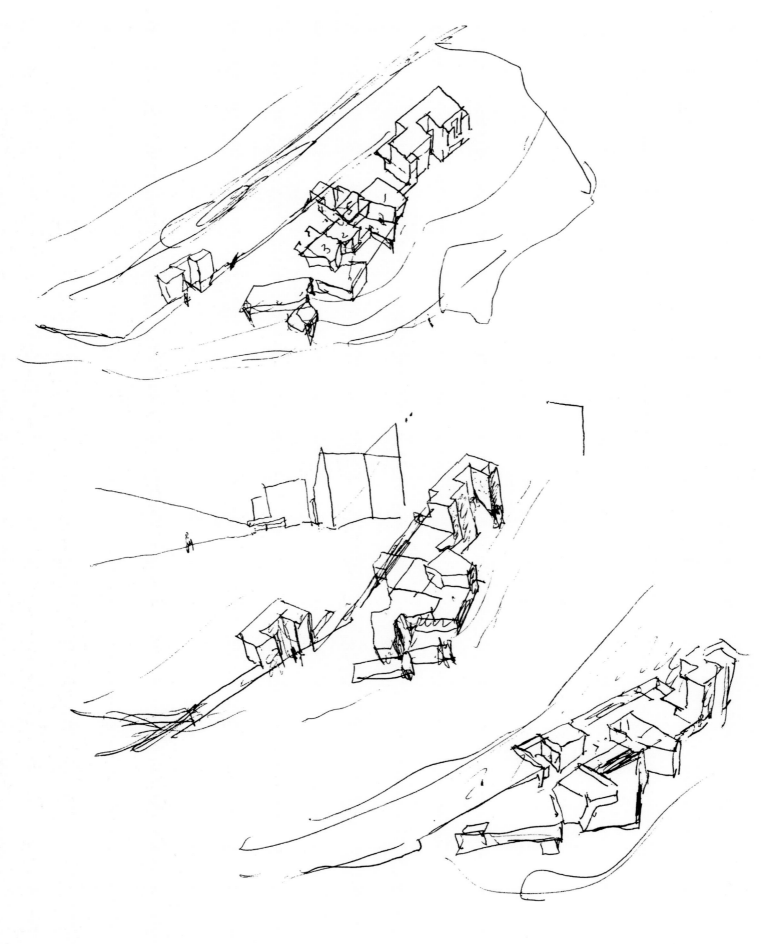

506
3.02

112   Volume aggregation studies.
113   Detail showing the complex geometry of the house.

114　Partial view of the main sitting room from
the dining room.
115　One of the few windows that faces the
sea directly.

116

ADEGA MAYOR WINERY

Campo Maior, Portugal 2003–2006

It is not easy to find an opportunity to build within such a beautiful, pristine landscape. It is also an enormous responsibility.

The Nabeiro Group winery in Campo Maior, a town in eastern Portugal, lies close to but detached from its industrial complex. The site — already accessible by road — was a compacted clay outcrop that had been dug out and used as a rubbish dump. The integrity of the natural landscape has been enhanced and ordered by the client, which has maintained the region's agricultural activity by planting cork, oaks and vineyards. Such were the defining characteristics of the project, combined with knowledge of the local architecture.

The rectangle of 40 × 120 meters (131 × 394 ft) of the winery, set into the pit, rises 9 meters (30 ft) with almost blind walls. At the southwestern extreme is the entrance for visitors and an access point for cargo, with an additional storey giving way to a panoramic terrace. At the opposite end is the delivery pier, and in the space between, there is a complex production area and a shaded storage area.

116 Volumetric studies with various solutions for the main facade.

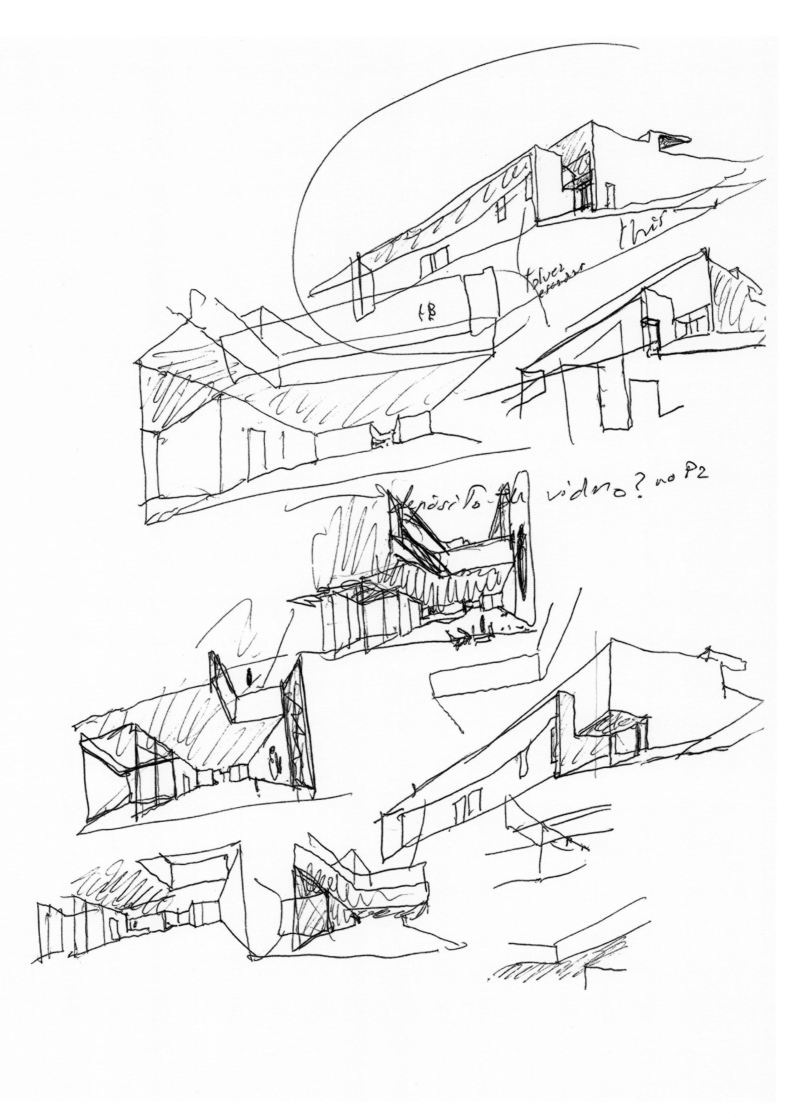

118 Studies for the interior and exterior of the
access area.
119 The entire volume seen from the west.

120 Detail of the main entrance.
121 Top: Distant view of the southeast elevation, with the newly planted vineyard in the foreground. Centre and Bottom: Views from the west and southwest.

122　Studies for the main entrance.
123　View from the south, showing the main entrance
in the foreground and the vehicle ramp bordering the
southeast elevation.

ADEGA MAYOR WINERY

124 Northeast elevation.
125 The canopy of the front facade frames a view
of the surrounding landscape.

125

ADEGA MAYOR WINERY

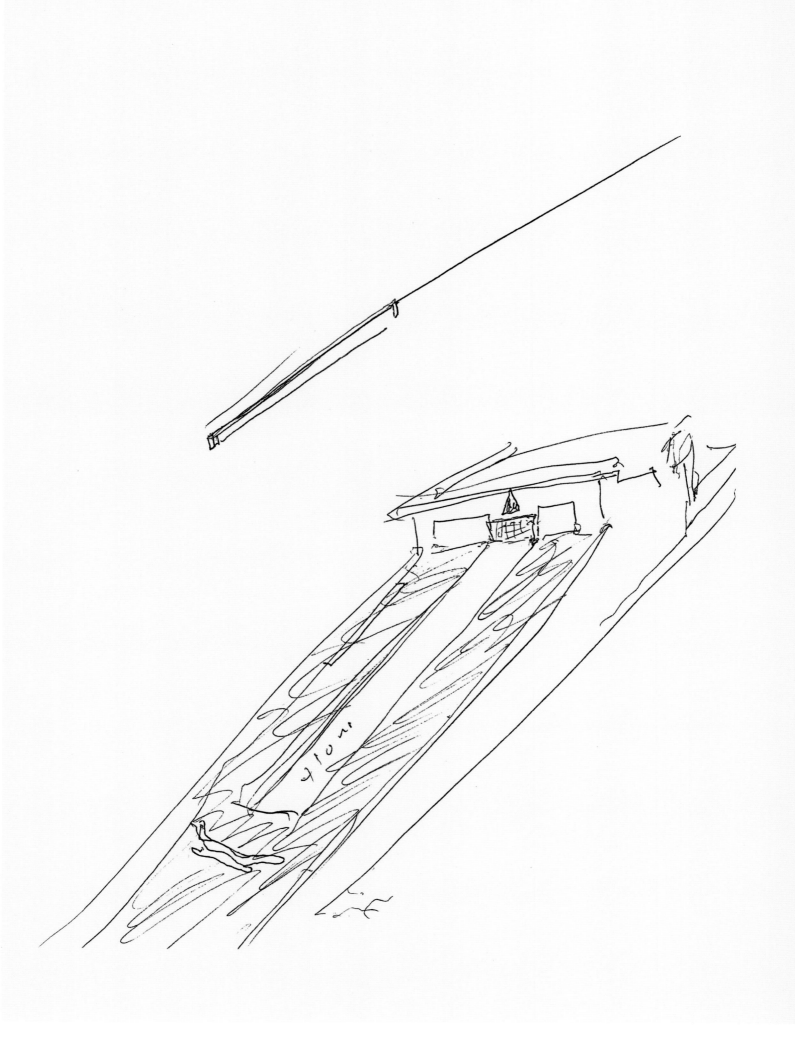

126   Sketch of the overall volume from the north.
127   Grass covering and a pool on the roof terrace
help improve the thermal performance of the building.

ADEGA MAYOR WINERY

128   Sketches of the double-height interior
circulation space.
129   Top: Double-height circulation space.
Bottom: Cellar.

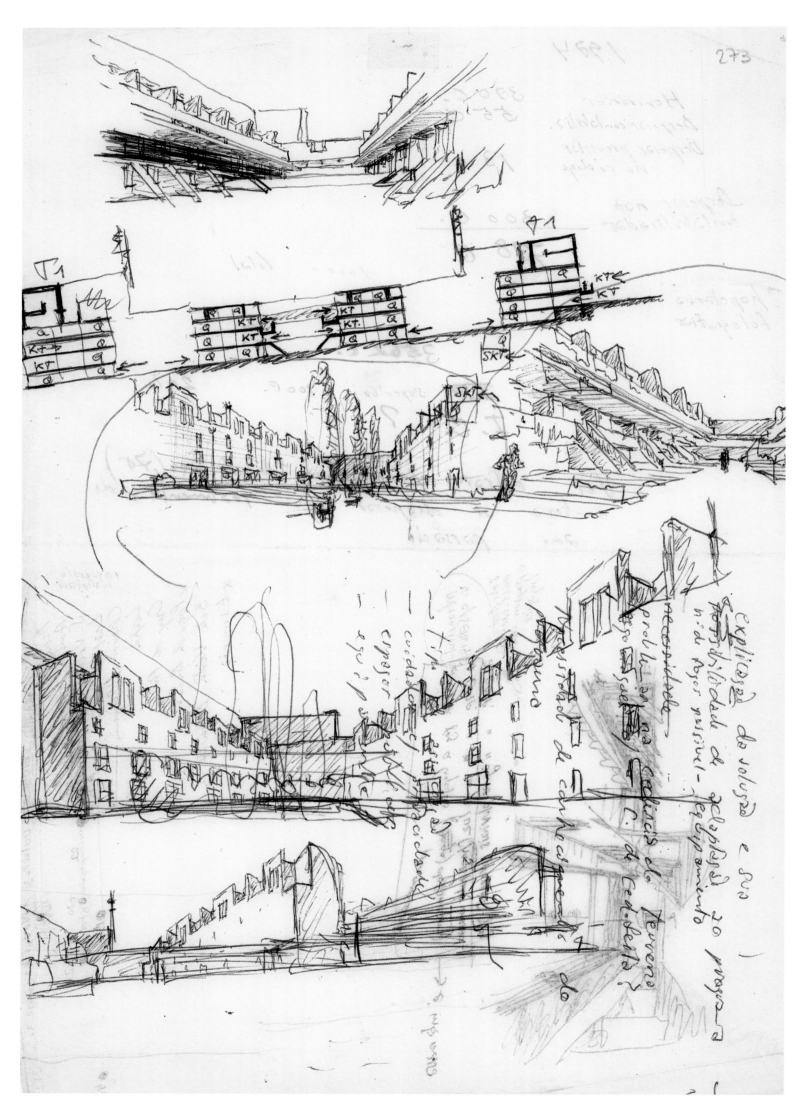

SAAL BOUÇA SOCIAL HOUSING

Porto, Portugal 1972–2006

The conclusion of SAAL Bouça was almost a surprise. Still, hope was never completely lost, due in part to the continuous pressure from the residents of the houses that were not finished in the first phase. After a thirty-year pause, the commitment of the Confederação Cooperativa Portuguesa (Federation of Cooperatives) was crucial to the decision of the Câmara Municipal do Porto (Municipality of Porto) and the Instituto Nacional da Habitacão (National Institute of Housing) to finish the work.

In addition to building the second phase, the project included refurbishing roughly one-third of the existing houses. It was not easy to convince residents to part with renovations or additions previously made to their homes. Many felt as if they were giving up the 'magnificent isolation' in which they lived, in the middle of the city — albeit in a degraded environment and in fear of rent increases.

A patient dialogue — one that made clear the obligation of maintaining the initial plan almost entirely, with few exceptions — was necessary. The purpose of preserving the built and inhabited houses as part of the overall project forced that decision. The dialogue included compromises and innovations, even of minor relevance. The design review required the consideration of the resident population's evolution in relation to the original context before the revolution of 1974. At that time, it was unthinkable to need a garage, for example, or to be concerned about delimiting public and private spaces, and the requirements of the future regulations were impossible to predict.

The Bouça project was radically economical; it couldn't and, indeed, shouldn't have been anything else in 1974. Discussion of the project years later revealed the desire (and the possibility, however limited) for specific improvements in quality and comfort. It was necessary to meet these demands, some of them prompted by prejudices that came alongside the objective improvement of the quality of life. This was also a collaborative process undertaken with the participation of the resident families.

Once the work was completed, the market's reaction showed that this type of housing no longer corresponded to current trends in the demand for affordable housing — for good or evil. On the other hand, the homes were attractive to other sectors of the population: students, young professionals, and newly formed families — the protagonists of mobility in the contemporary city.

As the project progressed, the needs of the complex's inhabitants evolved, altering the ultimate design from its original plan. But there is now a Metro station in front of the complex, linking it with the rest of the city; a flow of people crosses the site; facilities are open in the surrounding streets; and there is an orderly garden, and cars, as in any housing project. It is not the perfect work. But is that essential?

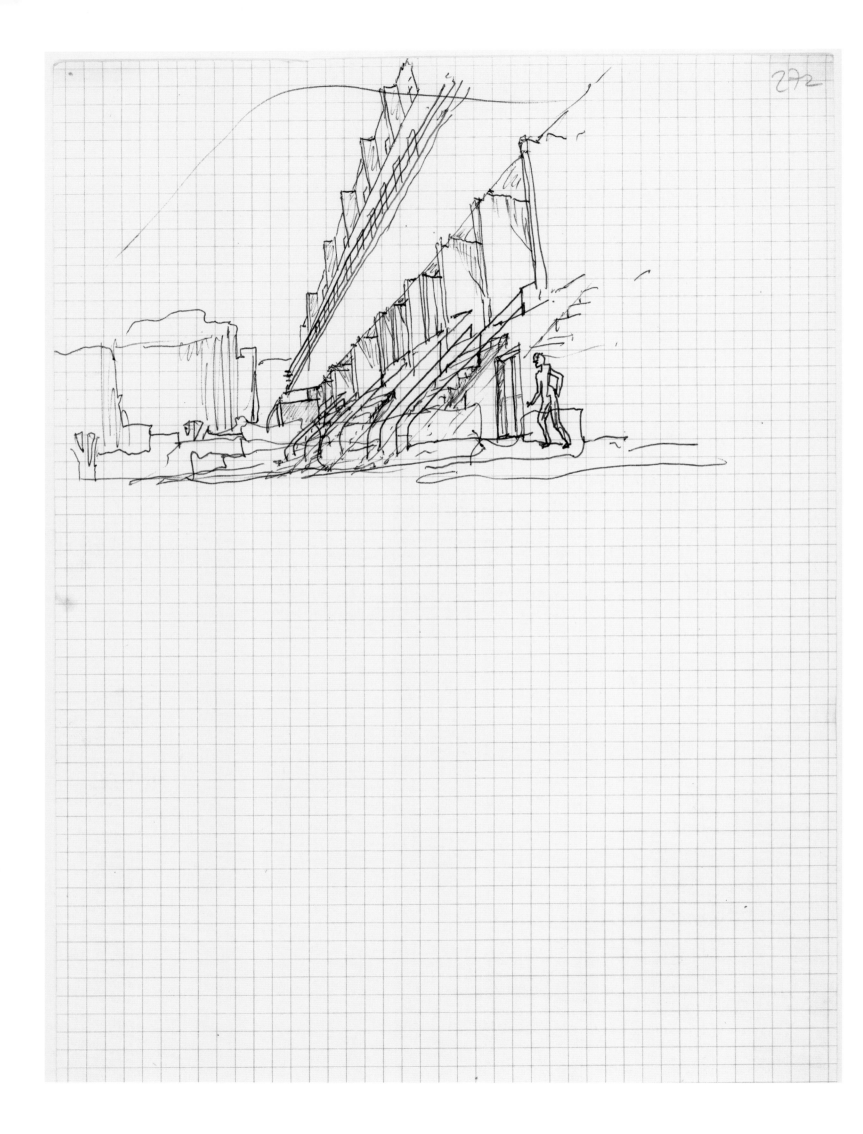

132   Sketch of one of the facades, with gallery
and staircases.
133   The courtyard is usually enlivened by children
and other residents.

134   Sketch of the overall volume and detail of a courtyard.
135   Top: View from the north of the concrete spine
wall and connecting gallery. The decision to include
a concrete wall here was made in part to help shield the
complex from the noise pollution of the nearby railway
tracks. Centre: Courtyard, showing the south side of the
concrete wall. Bottom: Communal facility at the southern
end of one of the housing blocks.

136   Preliminary sketch of the housing blocks,
with the communal facilities in the foreground.
137   Housing block entrance, with the communal
facility on the right–hand side.

138   Housing block entrance, with the stairs leading
to the first-floor gallery.
139   Top: Interior of a communal facility. Bottom:
Entrance corridor of a ground-floor apartment.

SAAL BOUÇA SOCIAL HOUSING

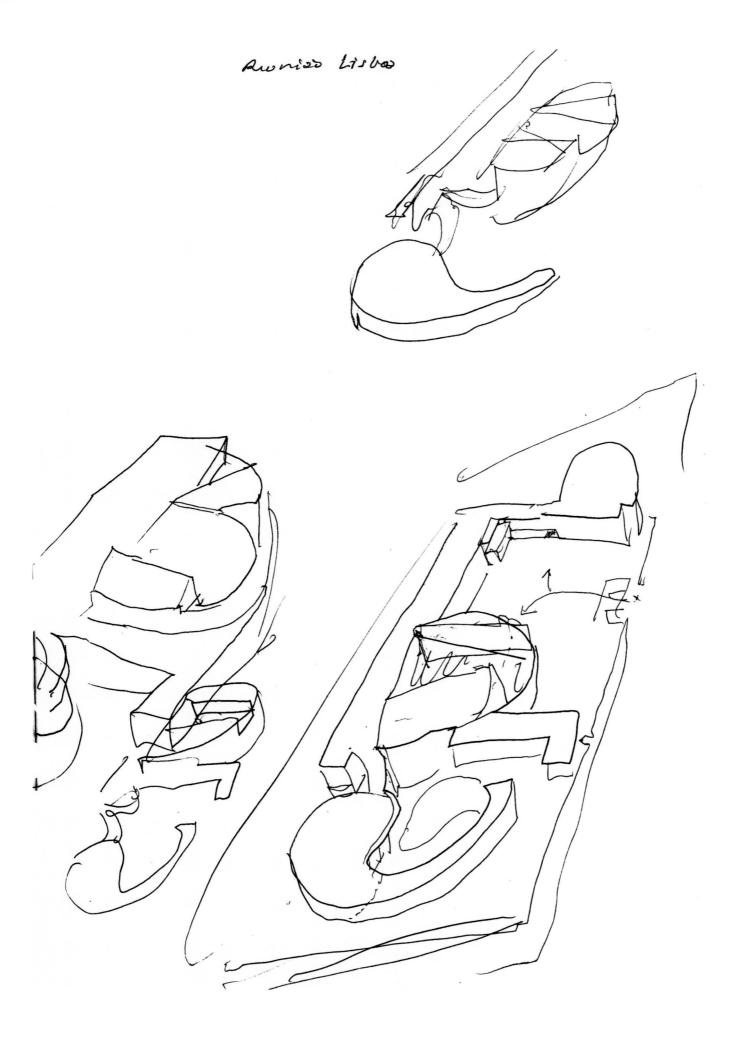

Reunião Lisboa

RIBERA SERRALLO SPORTS COMPLEX

Cornellà de Llobregat, Spain 2000–2006

Entrance to the complex is from the northeastern and southeastern sides of the plot, across a slight slope, limited by the multipurpose pavilion and a longitudinal volume from which it is possible to access both facilities. In the multipurpose pavilion, spectator stands may be accessed at the upper level from the main lobby, with one wall of stands able to retract, providing greater floor space. During everyday use, the athletes enter from the main hall, descending to the track level where there is also a longitudinal block of changing rooms, at the end of which a training pavilion will be constructed in the second building phase.

Access to the swimming pools is on the same level of the longitudinal block, one level below the main lobby. Changing rooms, lavatories and saunas are connected to the pools by a corridor. Spectators enter the aquatic area through a gallery at the main lobby level. Fitness rooms, spread across two levels, are accessed independently from a vertical core and share facilities and changing rooms with the swimming pools.

140   Preliminary isometric studies of the project.

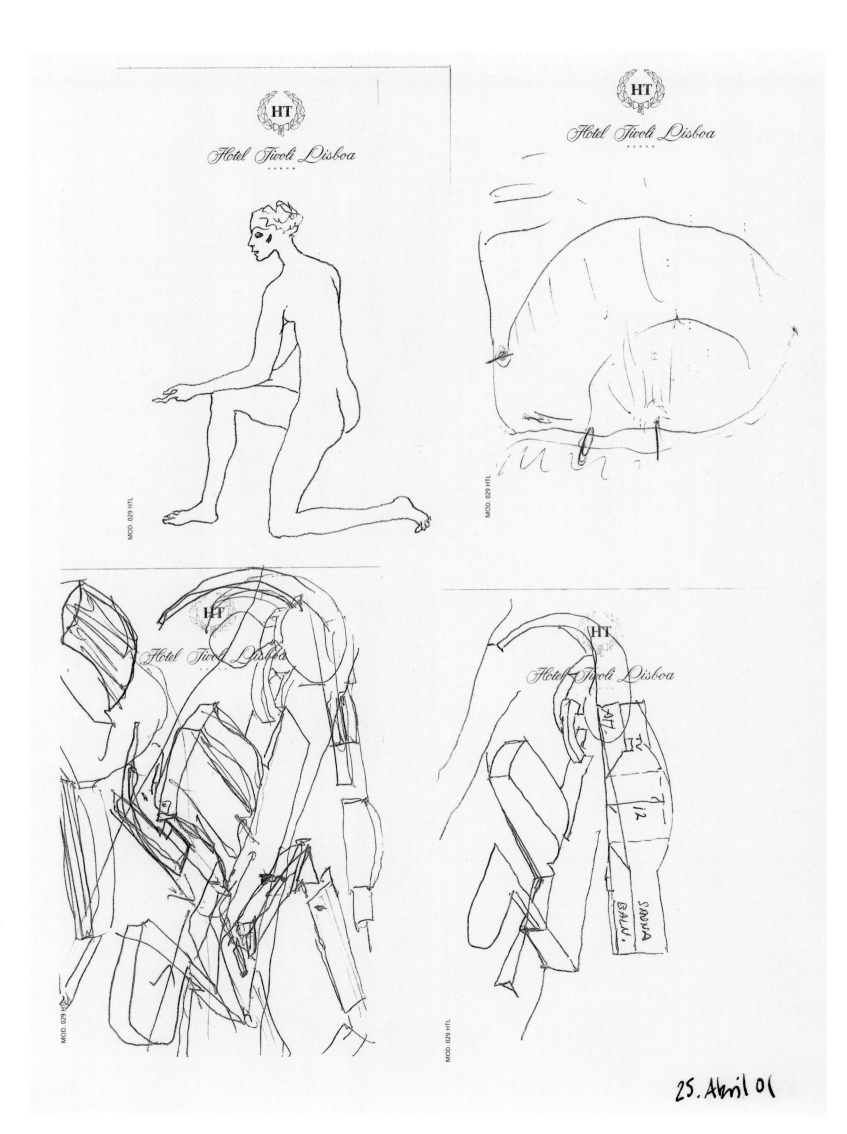

25. Abril 01

142 Preliminary studies.
143 Northeast elevation.

RIBERA SERRALLO SPORTS COMPLEX

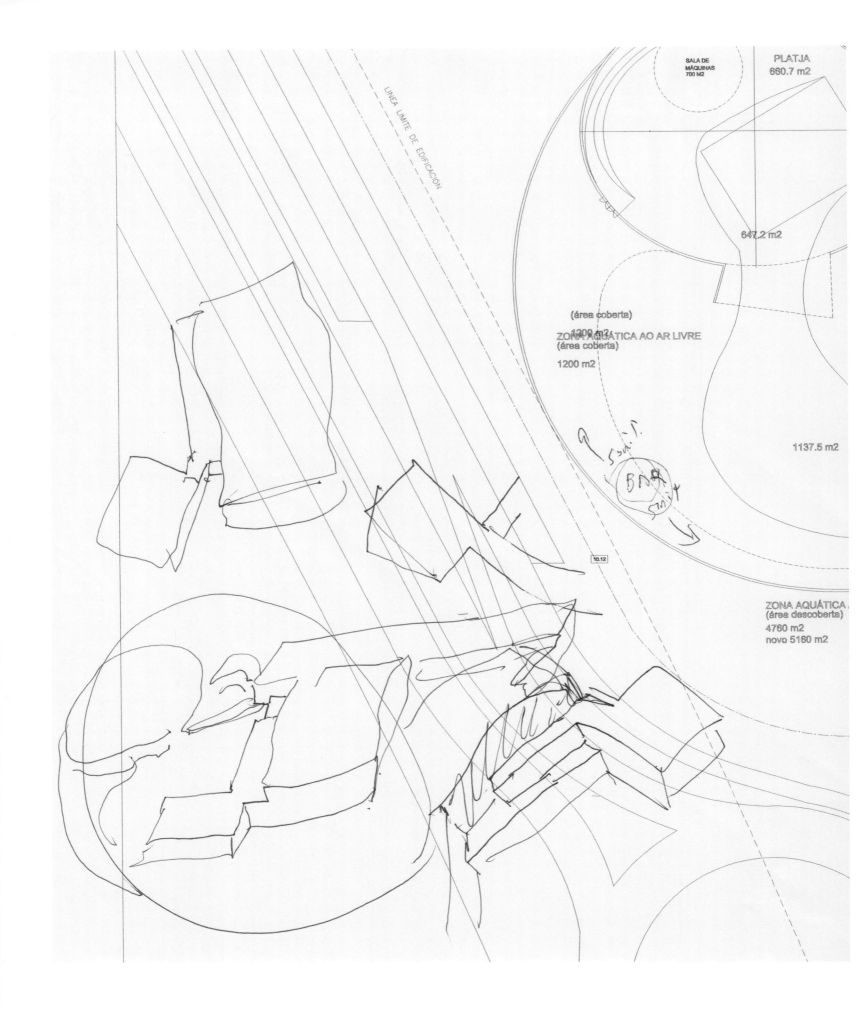

SALA DE
MÁQUINAS
700 M2

PLATJA
660.7 m2

647.2 m2

(área coberta)
1200 m2

ZONA AQUÁTICA AO AR LIVRE
(área coberta)

1200 m2

1137.5 m2

10.12

ZONA AQUÁTICA
(área descoberta)
4760 m2
novo 5160 m2

LINEA LIMITE DE EDIFICACIÓN

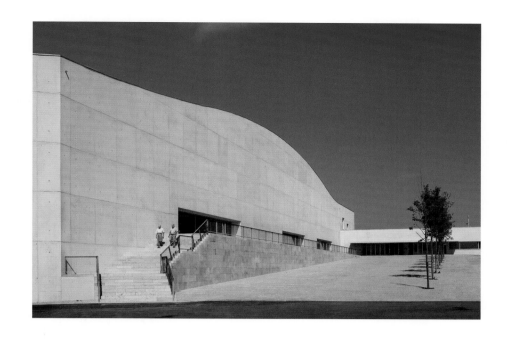

144   Preliminary studies.
145   Top: The multipurpose pavilion seen from
the east, with the main entrance in the background.
Centre: Outdoor swimming pool and southwest
elevation of the pavilion, seen from the south.
Bottom: The volume of the indoor swimming pool
and curved porch, seen from the east.

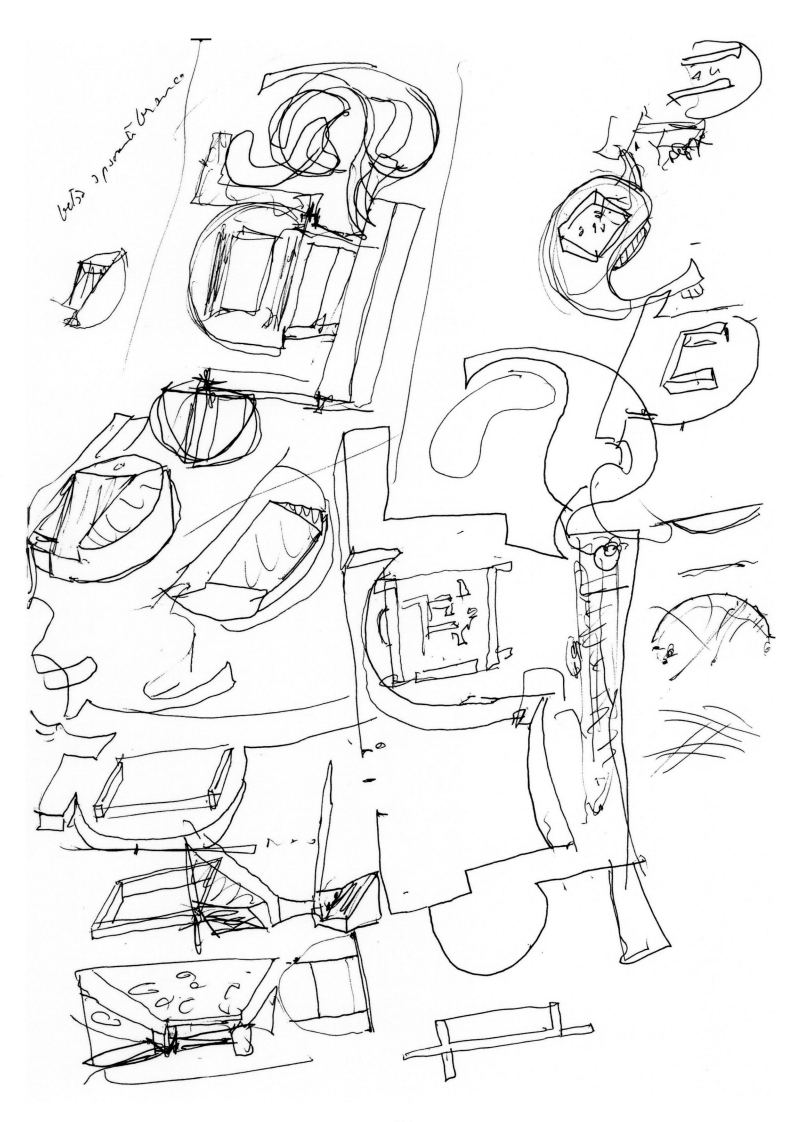

146

146   Studies for the indoor and outdoor swimming pools.
147   Overview of the indoor swimming pool building,
with its curved porch embracing the outdoor pool.

148   The main corridor connects the reception area
with the swimming pools and the pavilion.
149   Interior of the pavilion.

RIBERA SERRALLO SPORTS COMPLEX

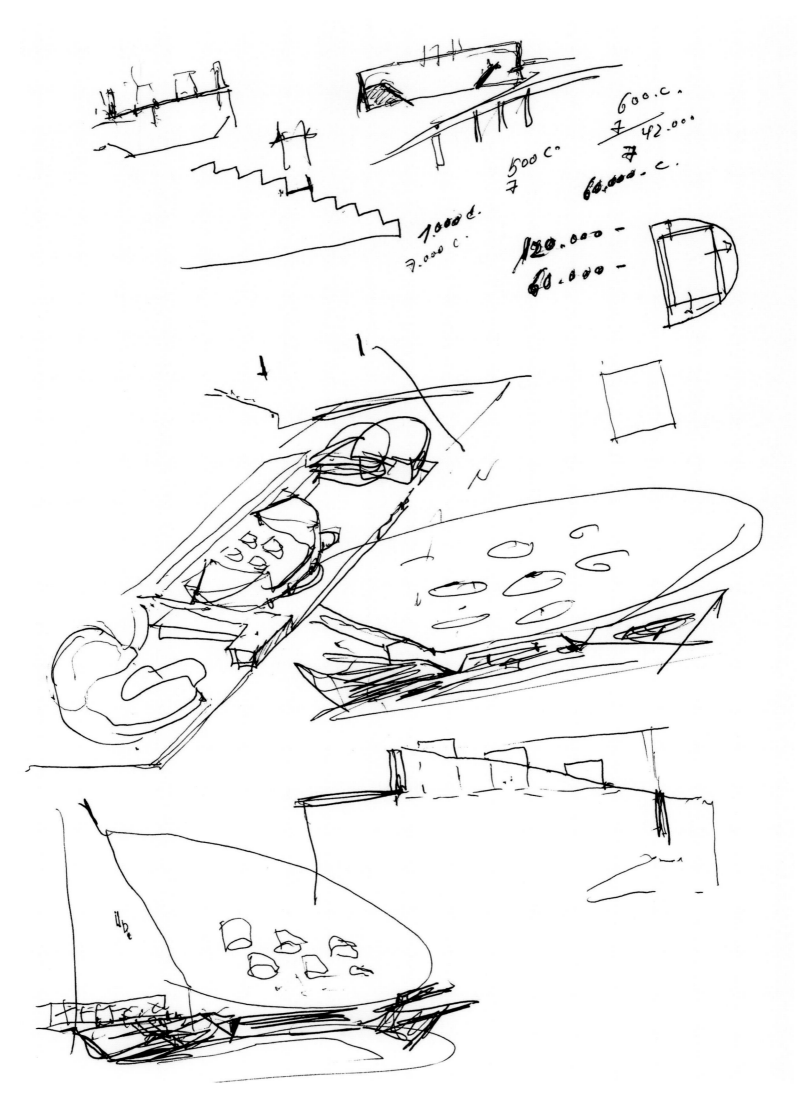

600.c.

500 C° 42.000

7.000 C. 60.000-c.

7.000 c. 120.000 -

60.000 -

150   Studies for the indoor swimming pool.
151   Overview of the indoor swimming pool with its
large, curved ramp.

VMD HOUSE AND ART GALLERY

Oudenburg, Belgium 1997—2003

This project involved the refurbishment of an old farmhouse. The volumes with high, steeply pitched roofs are distributed over flat ground on an immense plain fairly close to the sea. Agricultural activity continues there, although more modern practices and technologies are used now than in years past. The project appears to be very simple, but it was actually quite complex, owing to the juxtaposition of languages and because it brings together a house, an art gallery and farm buildings.

The three existing buildings arranged around a reception area were refurbished. Together with a new L-shaped residential volume, they define a second courtyard. One of the restored buildings, renovated internally as a single open space, was designated by the owners to hold exhibitions.

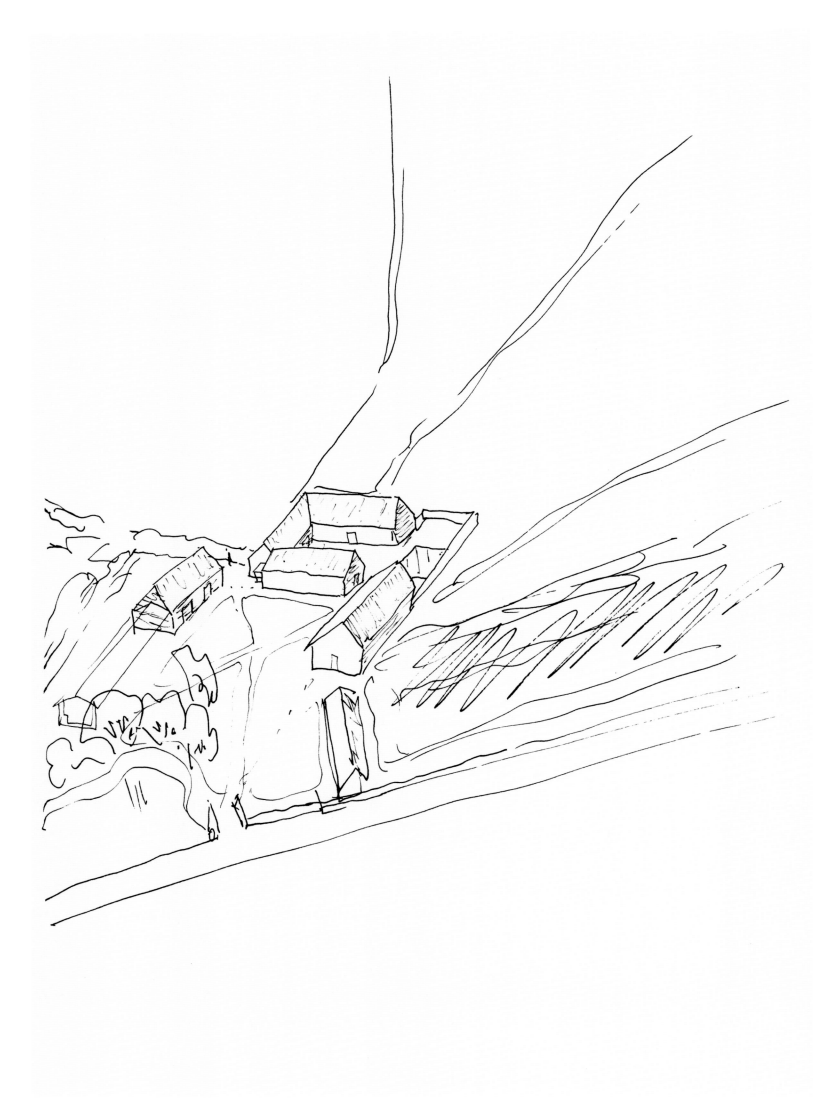

154   Overview of the complex.
155   The exteriors of the new volumes are mainly wrapped with cedar, and lead was chosen for the roofing material. The featured sculpture is *One Bronze Figure* (1993) by Juan Muñoz.

156   Plan scheme, with various interior and exterior sketches.
157   Top: The house seen from the southwest. Centre: South
elevation. Bottom: West elevation.

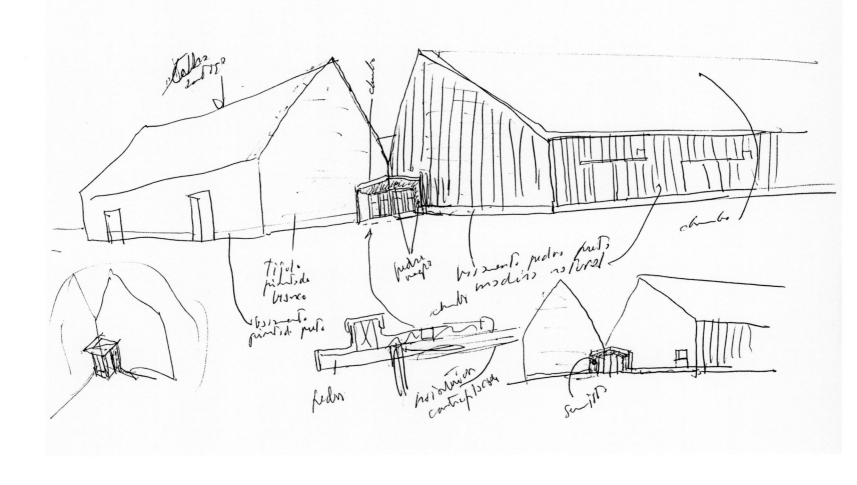

158 Studies for the main entrance.
159 Main entrance.

VMD HOUSE AND ART GALLERY

160 Plan with interior details.
161 Detail of the protruding window of the sitting room.

162   Sketches of the sitting room.
163   Top: Interior view of the protruding window. Centre:
Opposite view of the sitting room, showing the chimney.
Bottom: Dining room, with the sitting room beyond.

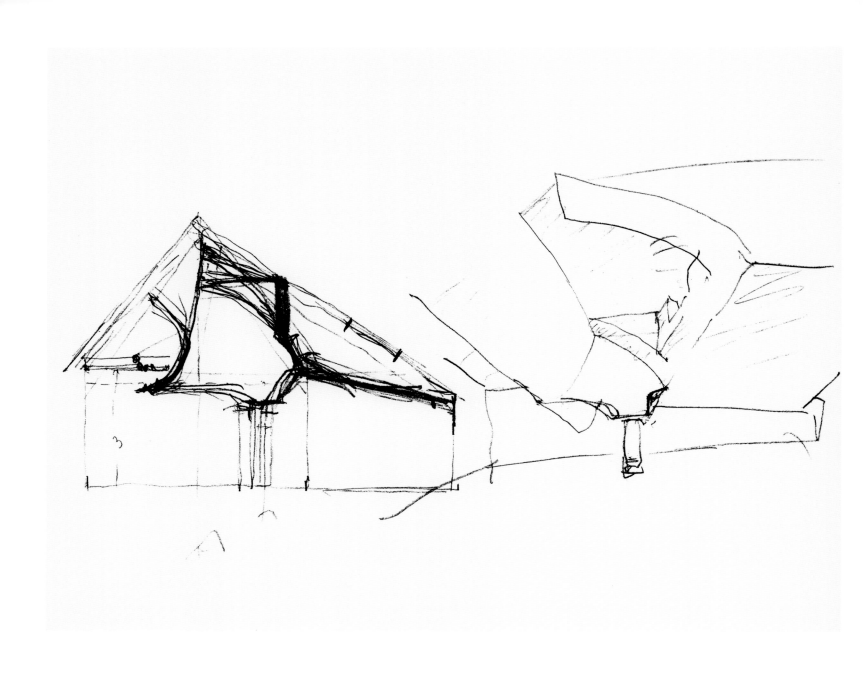

164 Studies for the exhibition gallery lighting.
165 The exhibition gallery (top) and the gallery's entrance (bottom). The works featured here (*E-Max*, 2002) were created by sculptor Panamarenko.

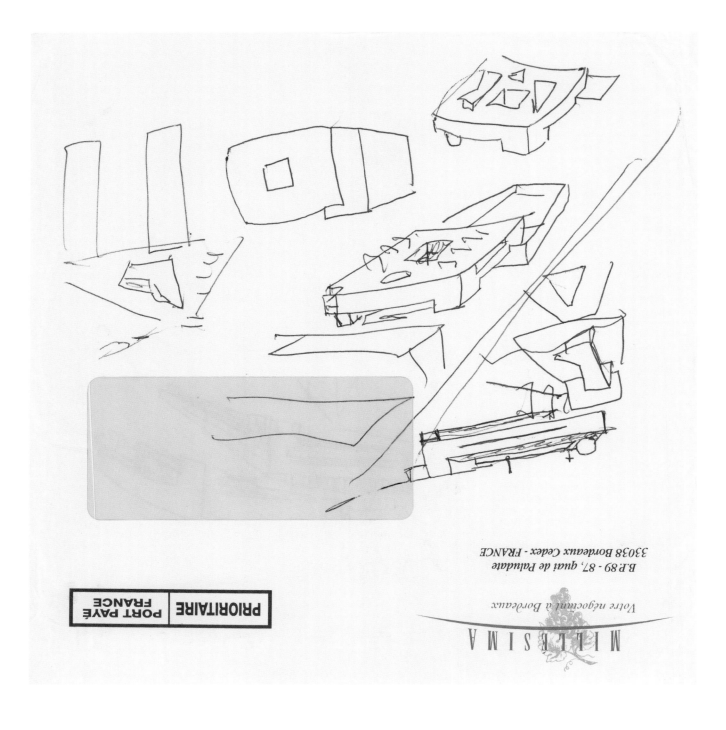

PRIORITAIRE
PORT PAYÉ FRANCE

MILLESIMA

Votre négociant à Bordeaux

B.P.89 - 87, quai de Paludate
33038 Bordeaux Cedex - FRANCE

MUNICIPAL LIBRARY

Viana do Castelo, Portugal, 2001–2007

Viana do Castelo's public library is built on a strip of land on the northern bank of the River Lima. It is part of a masterplan for Viana's riverfront, designed in 1995 by the eminent architect Fernando Távora. The plan also included two buildings (already constructed), framing Praça da Liberdade and the Monumento ao 25 de Abril (Monument to the 25 April), as well as the construction of a multipurpose hall and the landscaping of the outdoor spaces. The setting of the building was agreed with Prof. Távora and the other designers (the architects Eduardo Souto de Moura, José Bernardo Távora [the professor's son] and Adalberto Dias).

Set at the extreme eastern end of the planned sequence of structures, the library consists of a volume 45 meters (148 ft) square, with a central void 20 meters (66 ft) square. This volume extends eastwards at ground level via an L-shaped volume and by low walls that frame the riverfront garden.

Public access to the lobby is from the space defined by the higher volume and the central void, which is 0.6 meters (just over 2 ft) above the ground level outside. Four steps and a ramp negotiate the height difference. The staff area may be accessed through the public lobby or a shelter at the eastern end of the library, designated as the library car park. The technical rooms and boiler are next to this shelter.

The architectural expression derives primarily from the following characteristics:
– As many vantage points of the river, made possible through the building's elevation, with support at the east and west ends by two L-shaped pillars and the area constructed on the ground floor, respectively;
– Orthogonality in plan and elevation;
– The prevalence of large horizontal openings, complemented by rooflights;
– Solar protection or proper orientation of all openings;
– An exterior of white concrete clad at the base with faceted stone;
– Volumetric definition intentionally conditioned by the dialogue between garden and structure.

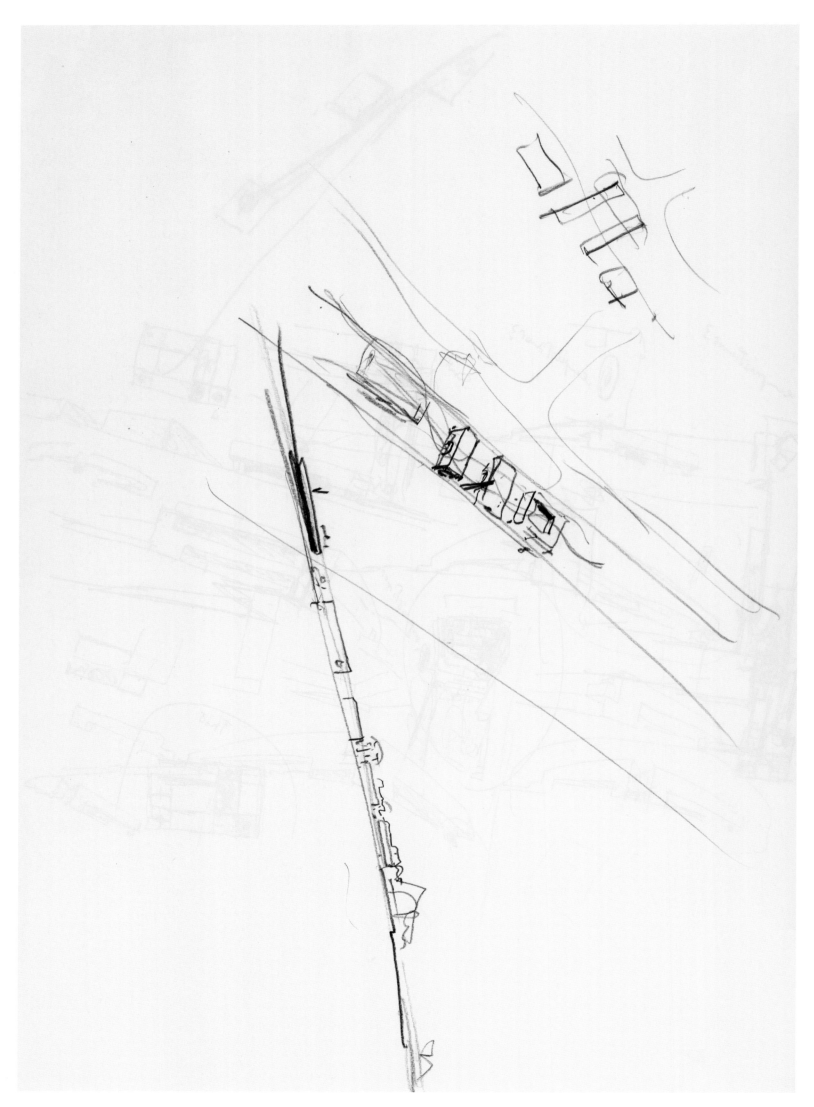

168 Site plan and sketch of riverfront view.
169 View from the opposite side of the Lima River,
with the chapel of São Lourenço in the foreground.

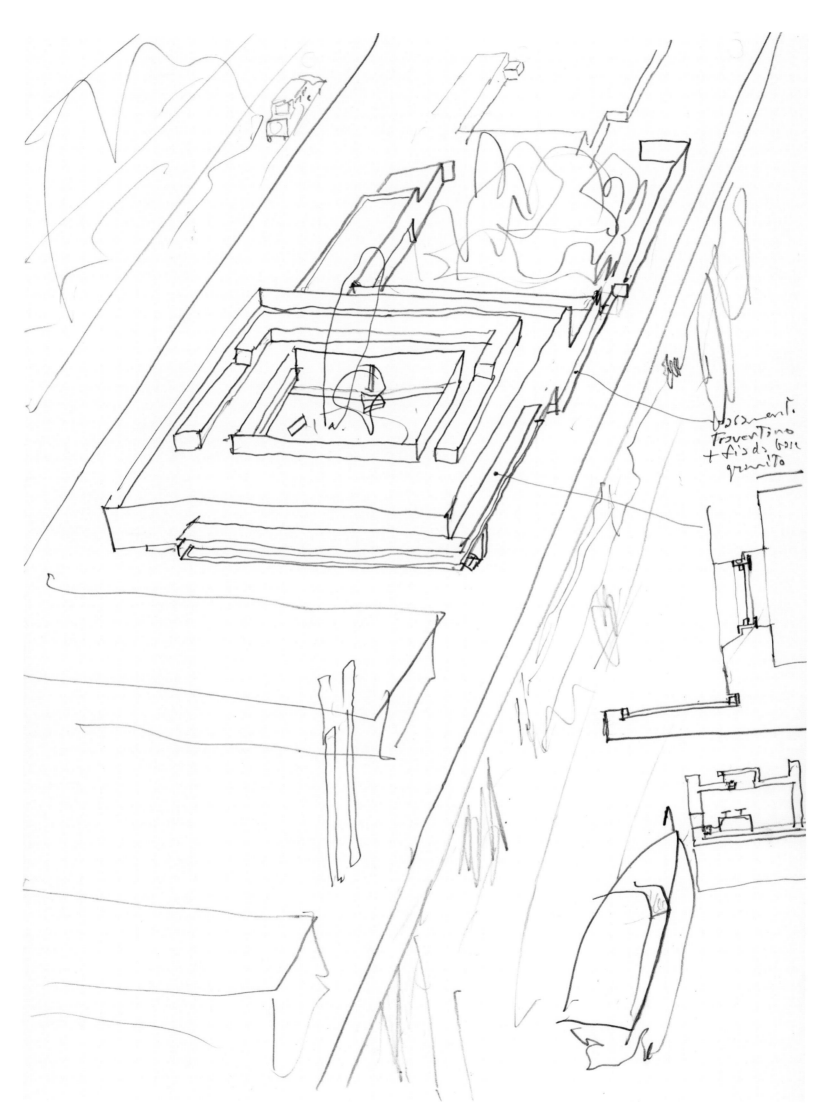

basamenti.
Travertino
+ fis di base
granito

170 Overview and construction details.
171 Top: First-floor terrace with the river in the background. Centre: Open courtyard. Bottom: Partial view of the southwest elevation, with the courtyard and riverside promenade beyond.

MUNICIPAL LIBRARY

172   Study for the overall volume, with the edge
of the historic city centre on the left and the riverside
on the right.
173   Partial view of the southwest elevation, with
the historic centre in the background.

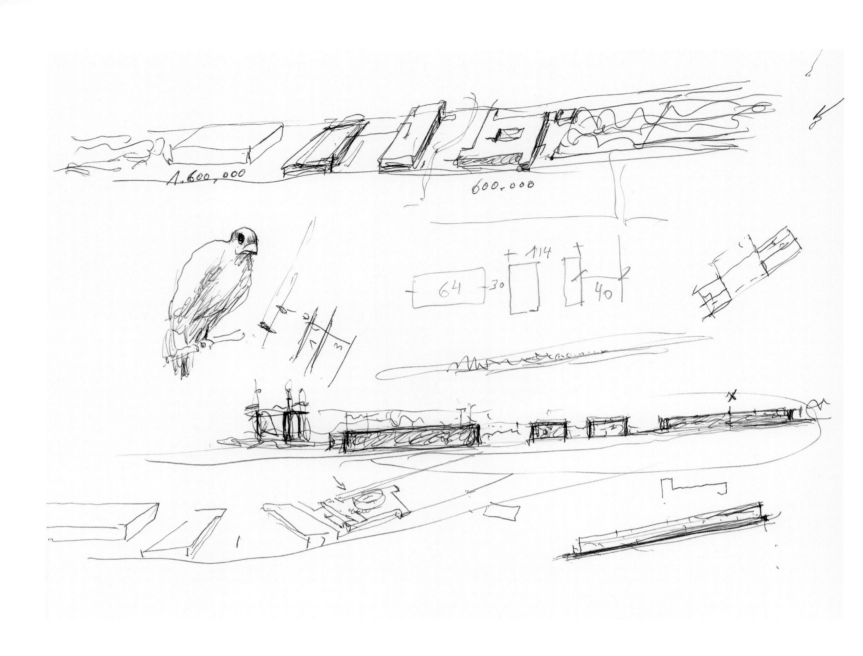

1.600,000

600,000

64   30   ↑14   40

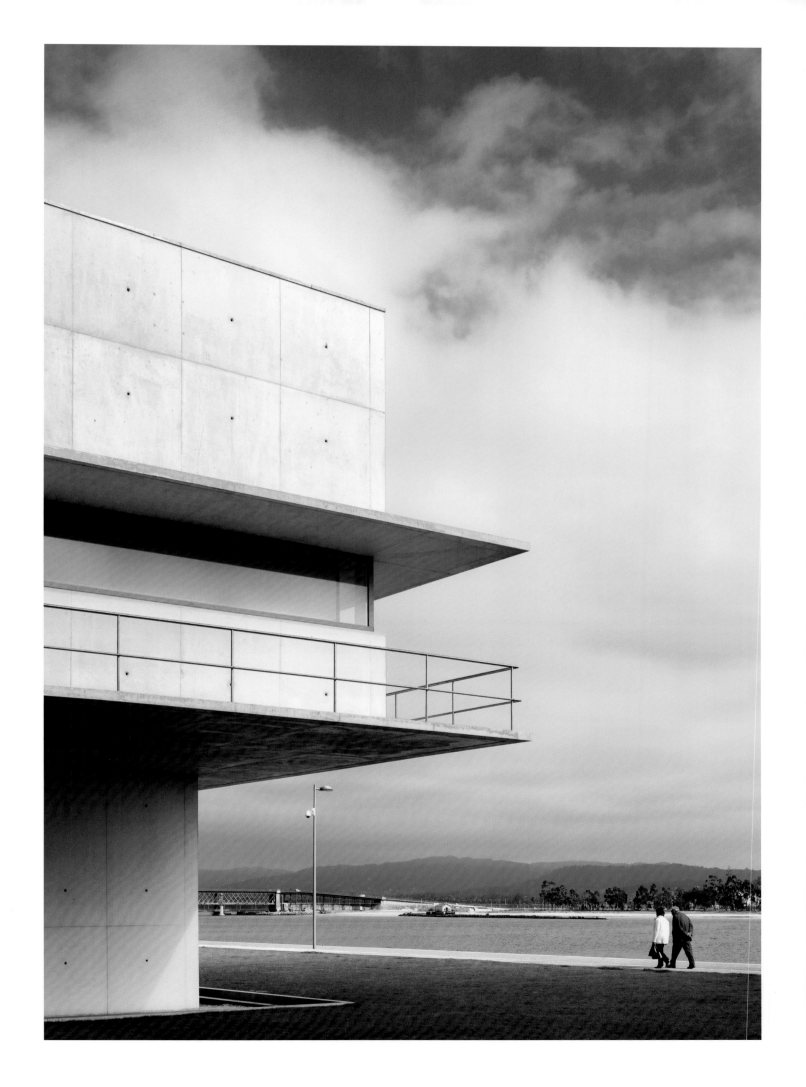

174   Site plan studies.
175   Detail of the south corner with wraparound balcony.

MUNICIPAL LIBRARY

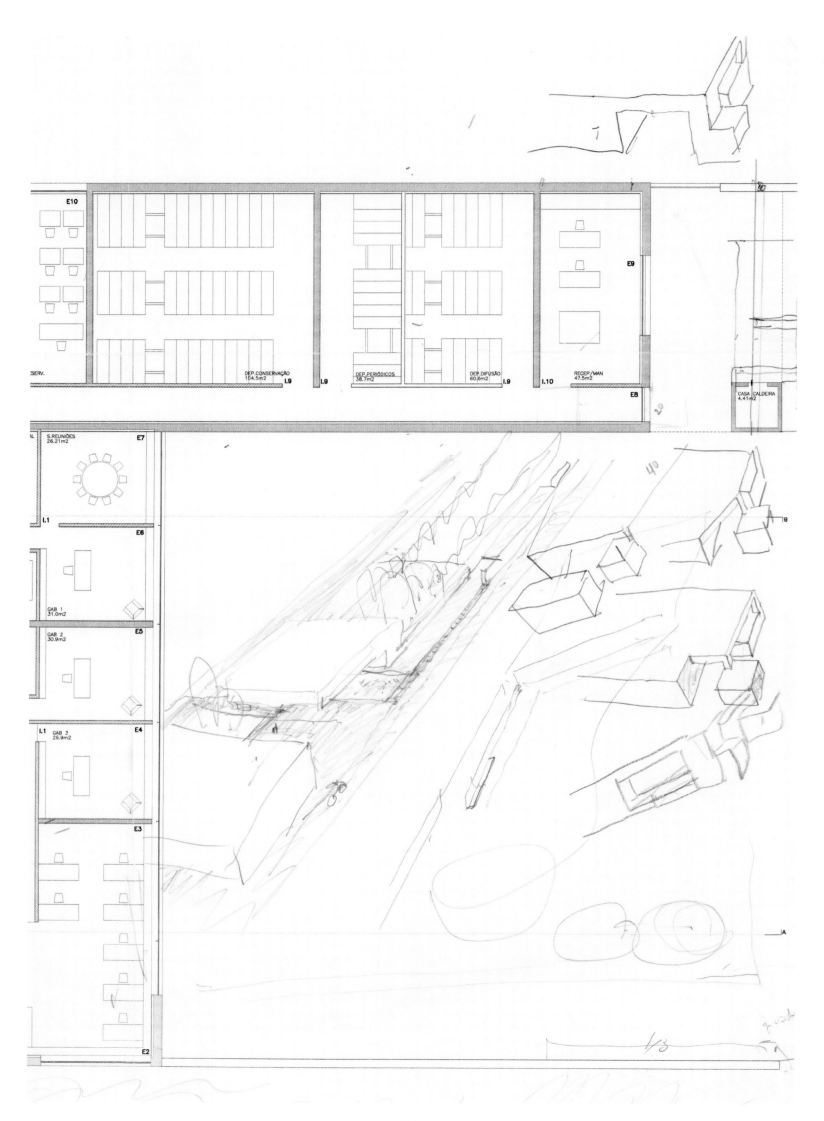

E10

SERV.

DEP.CONSERVAÇÃO
104.5m2   I.9

I.9

DEP.PERIÓDICOS
38.7m2

DEP.DIFUSÃO
60.6m2   I.9

RECEP/MAN
47.5m2

I.10

E9

E8

CASA CALDEIRA
4.41m2

AL   S.REUNIÕES
26.21m2

E7

I.1

E6

GAB 1
31.0m2

E5

GAB 2
30.9m2

I.1   GAB 3
26.9m2

E4

E3

E2

B

A

176   Volumetric sketches drawn on a fragment
of the first-floor plan.
177   Top: Main staircase connecting first and ground
floors. Centre: Reception desk in the entrance hall.
Bottom: Children's section of the library.

MUNICIPAL LIBRARY

178   Longitudinal view of the main reading space
with extended skylight.
179   Transverse view of the main reading room.

MUNICIPAL LIBRARY

IBERÊ CAMARGO
FOUNDATION MUSEUM

Porto Alegre, Brazil, 1998—2008

The Foundation was created to preserve and promote the works of the Brazilian painter Iberê Camargo (1914—1994). Provided by the government of Porto Alegre, the site upon which the building sits is relatively small, narrow and limited by the slope of an old quarry and a roadway that skirts the Guaíba River.

Given the constraints of the site, the museum had to develop in height. Above the ground-floor lobby are three floors of exhibition halls, all open to an atrium which extends the height of the building. In addition, small interconnected volumes house other parts of the programme, including teaching studios, cafe, offices, a small auditorium and a library. The archives, warehouses and technical areas occupy the basement, which also includes other facilities related to the ground floor of the attached volumes. The car park was built under the coastal road.

The facade of the main building is wavy, reflecting the shape of the escarpment that borders the plot. The exhibition rooms on the three upper floors are interconnected, forming an L-shape, limited by the central space. The vertical circulation includes stairs, lifts and a continuous ramp, partly inside and partly outside, swooping out in places from the mass of the building.

180   Study of the site.

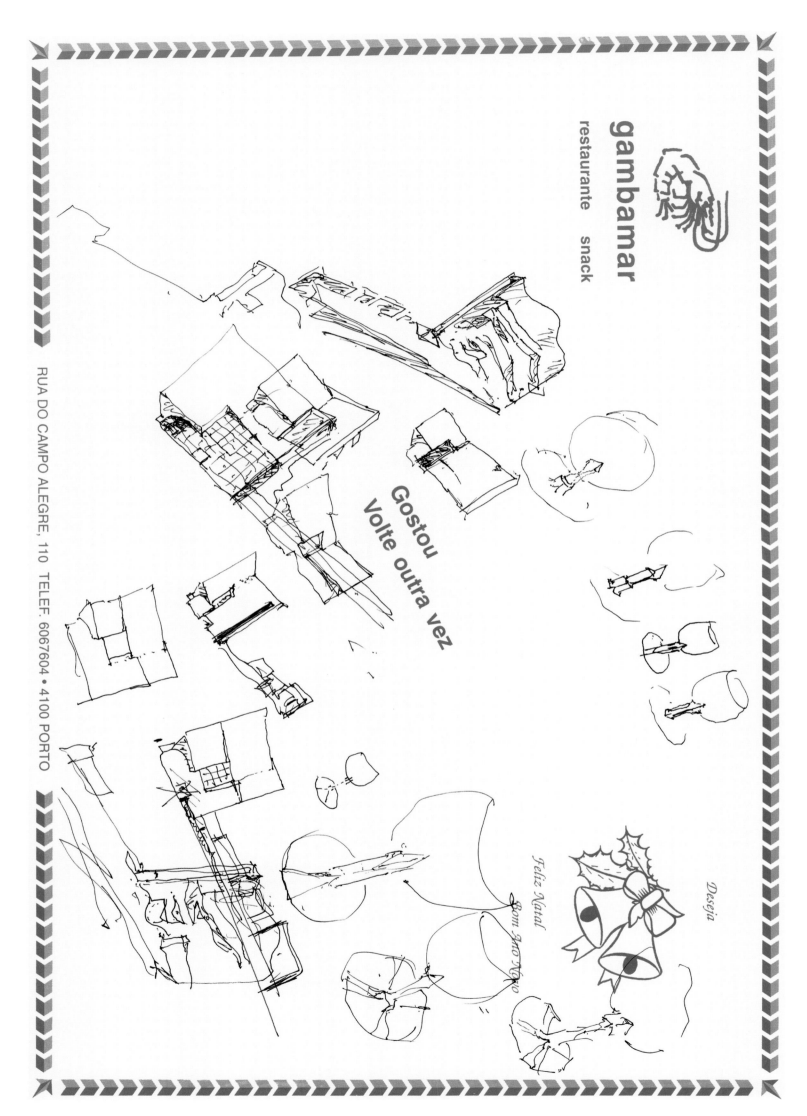

gambamar

restaurante   snack

Gostou
Volte outra vez

Feliz Natal
Bom Ano Novo

Deseja

RUA DO CAMPO ALEGRE, 110 TELEF. 6067604 • 4100 PORTO

182 First volumetric sketches drawn on a paper place mat.
183 The museum from the northeast, with the Guaíba river on the right.

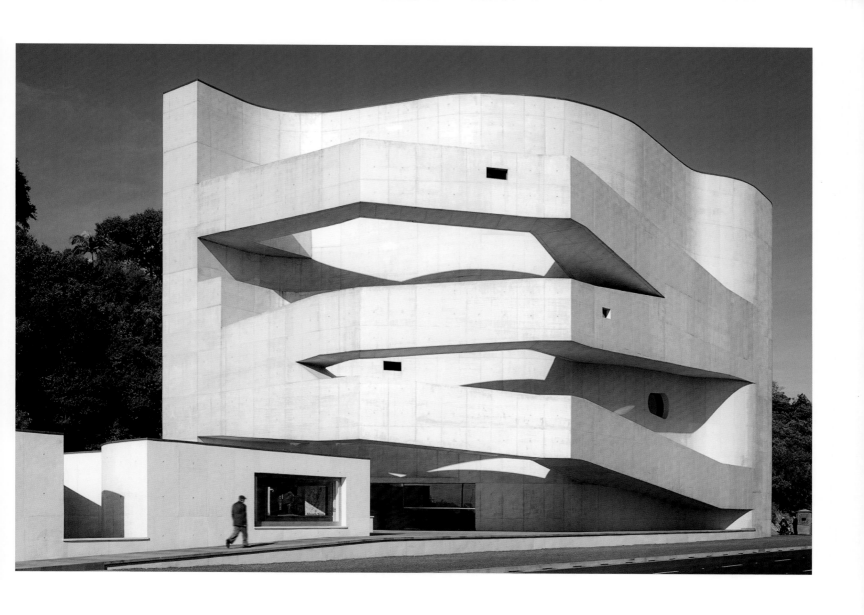

184   Sketch of the main volume.
185   North facade.

186   Main entrance, as seen from across Padre Cacique Avenue.
187   Top: Looking directly upward through the entrance courtyard. Bottom: Entrance courtyard with the river in the background.

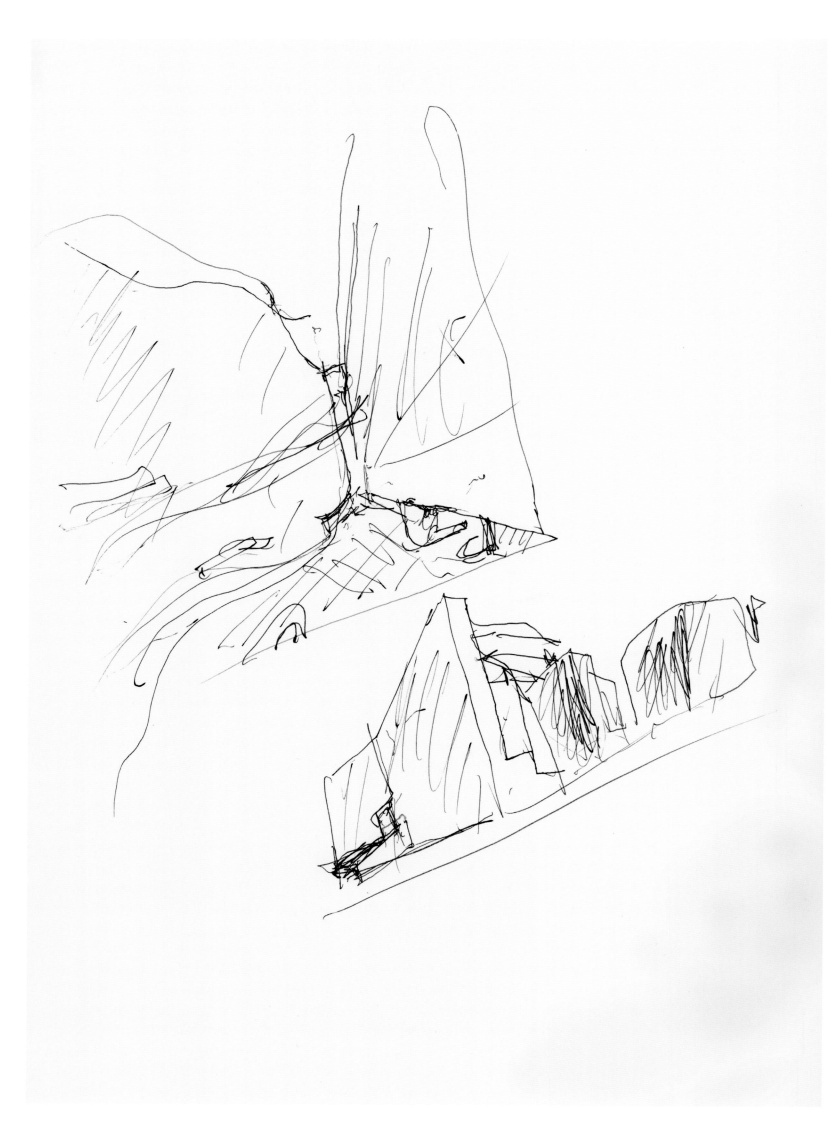

188   Sketches of the main central space and hillside
elevation.
189   Entrance courtyard, often described as an
'open lobby'.

190 Plan, sections and perspective view.
191 Interior of the entrance area.

192   Study for the main central space.
193   The ramp bordering the northern side of the central space.

IBERÊ CAMARGO FOUNDATION MUSEUM

194 and 195 The windows along the ramp grant
visitors sweeping views of the Porto Alegre riverfront.

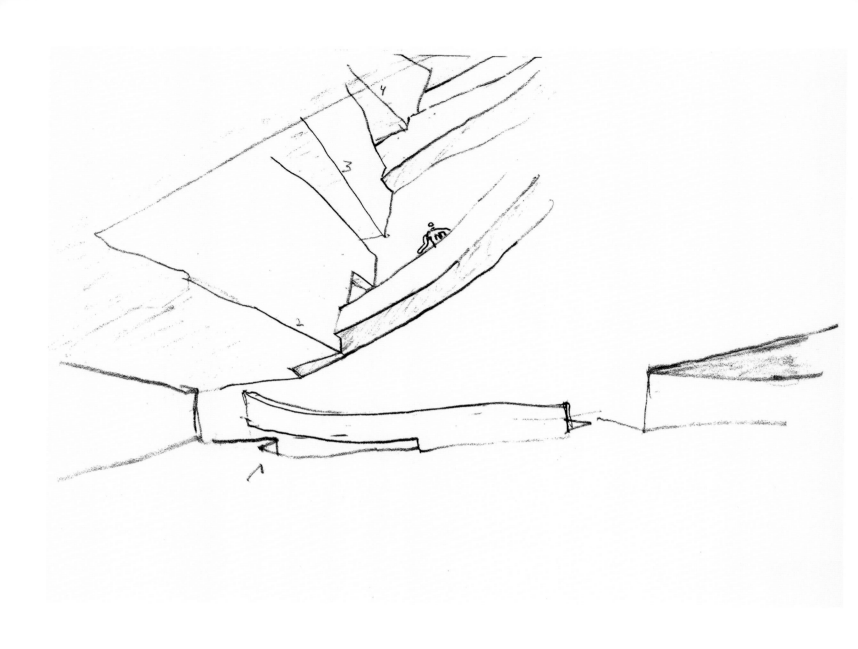

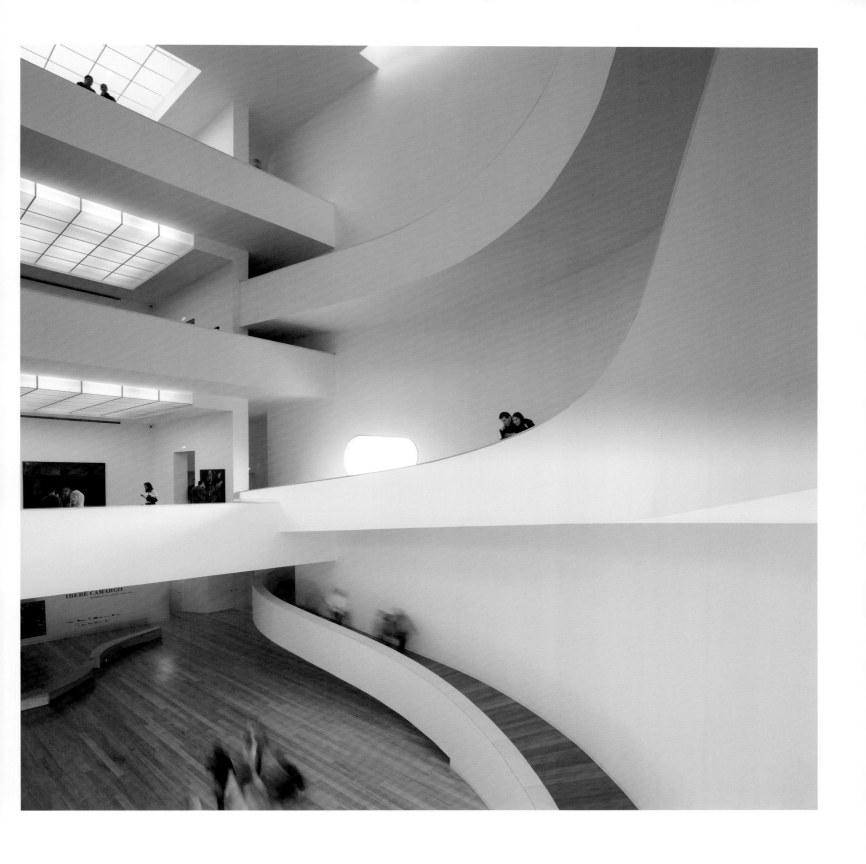

196 Sketch of the western side of the central space.
197 Partial view of the central space.

198   Part of the exhibition area is conceived as a series of
balconies overlooking the central space.
199   Top: Landing of the ramp on the top floor, with exhibition
spaces beyond. Bottom: The basement auditorium.

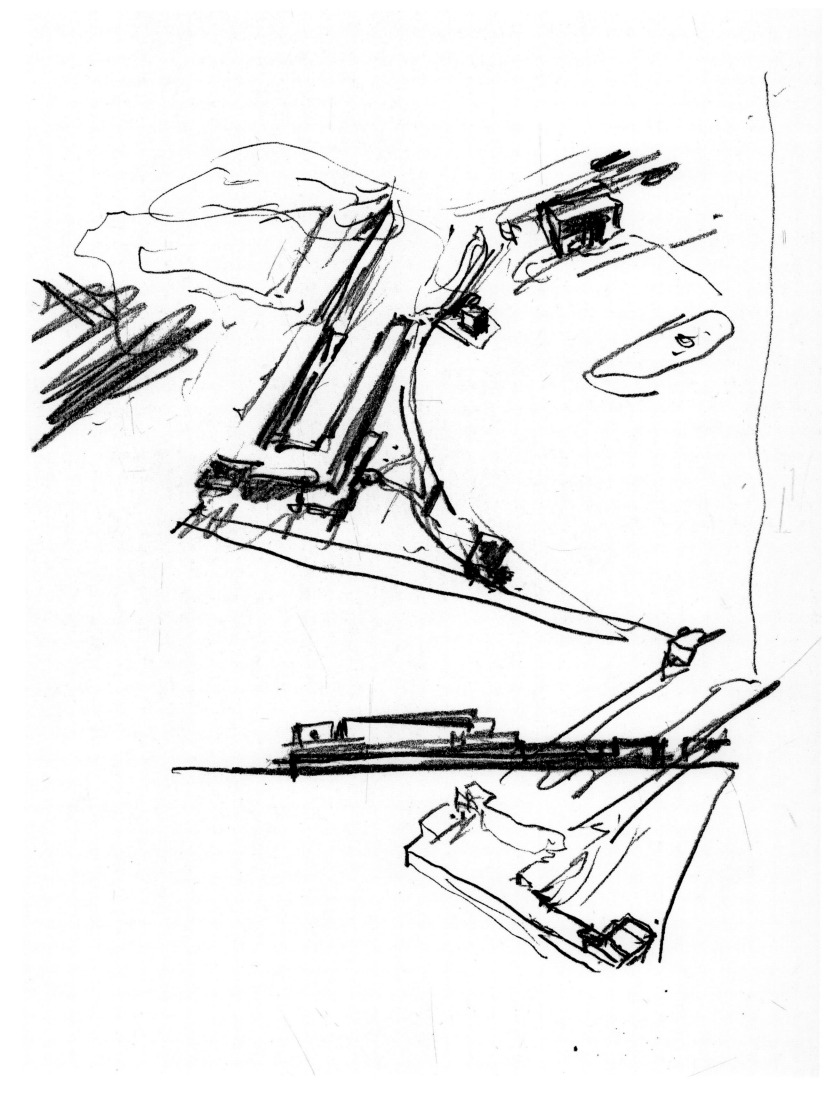

COLLEGE OF EDUCATION

Setúbal, Portugal, 1986–1994

This type of academic building requires a design approach that, although rigorous, allows great flexibility in the use and articulation of spaces. Hence the request for a very clear circulation system and a modular structure to facilitate later modifications of certain areas or the creation of new ones.

The complex is schematically an 'H', with two wings of two storeys, each framing the access path to the lobby, which is set perpendicular to them. This wide cross-space is the core area of the complex, where the circulation galleries begin and from where the most extensive parts of the programme can be accessed (canteen, the Centre for Documentation and Information and the Centre for Educational Resources). The amphitheatre, music room and gym adjoin the northwest elevation of the building and are accessed from the northern longitudinal gallery.

The school complex ends in the southwest with a long platform, raised slightly above the adjacent cultivated land and accessible from the existing southwestern pathway. Other areas of the programme (garage and services, guest house) stand as pavilions separated from the main building.

Special attention was paid to the savings that could be made during construction and to the economy of maintenance. In general terms, the strategy was to adopt a modular orthogonal system that ensures simplicity, economy and consistency of detail.

200 Sketches of the overall volume.

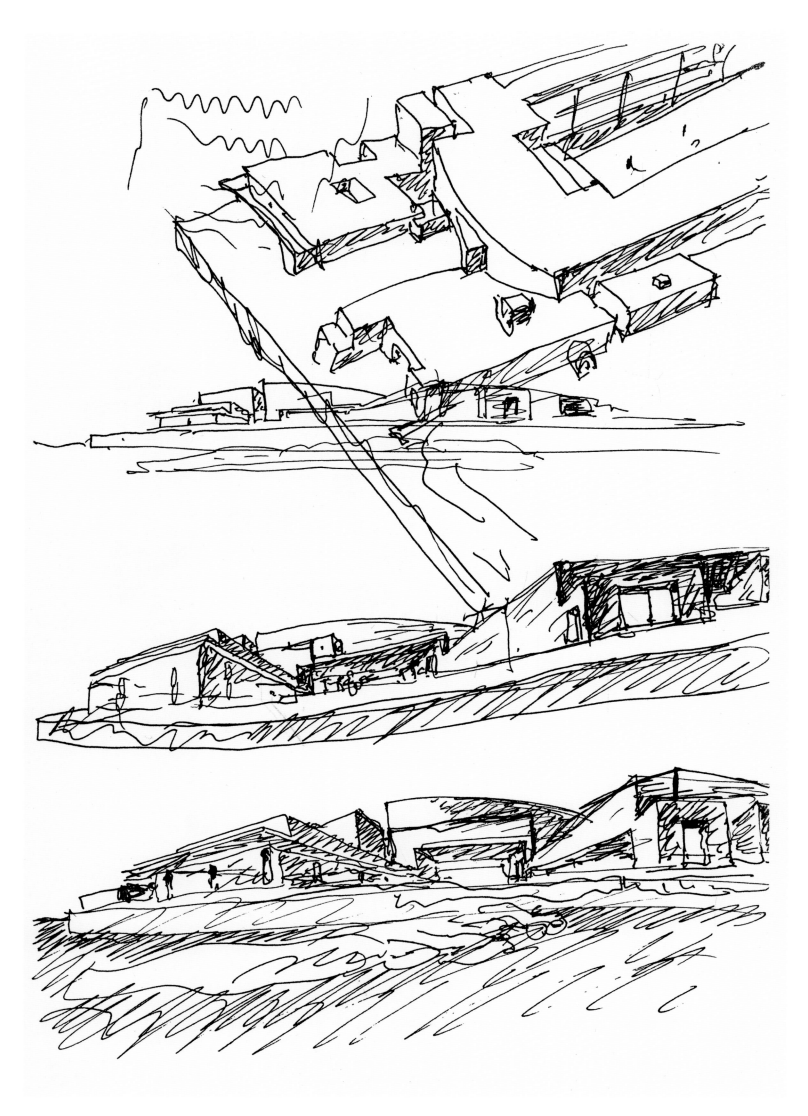

202 Studies for the courtyard in front of the
main entrance.
203 Top: Partial view of the complex from the south.
Centre: Southeast elevation with side entrance.
Bottom: South wing of the main building, facing the
inner courtyard.

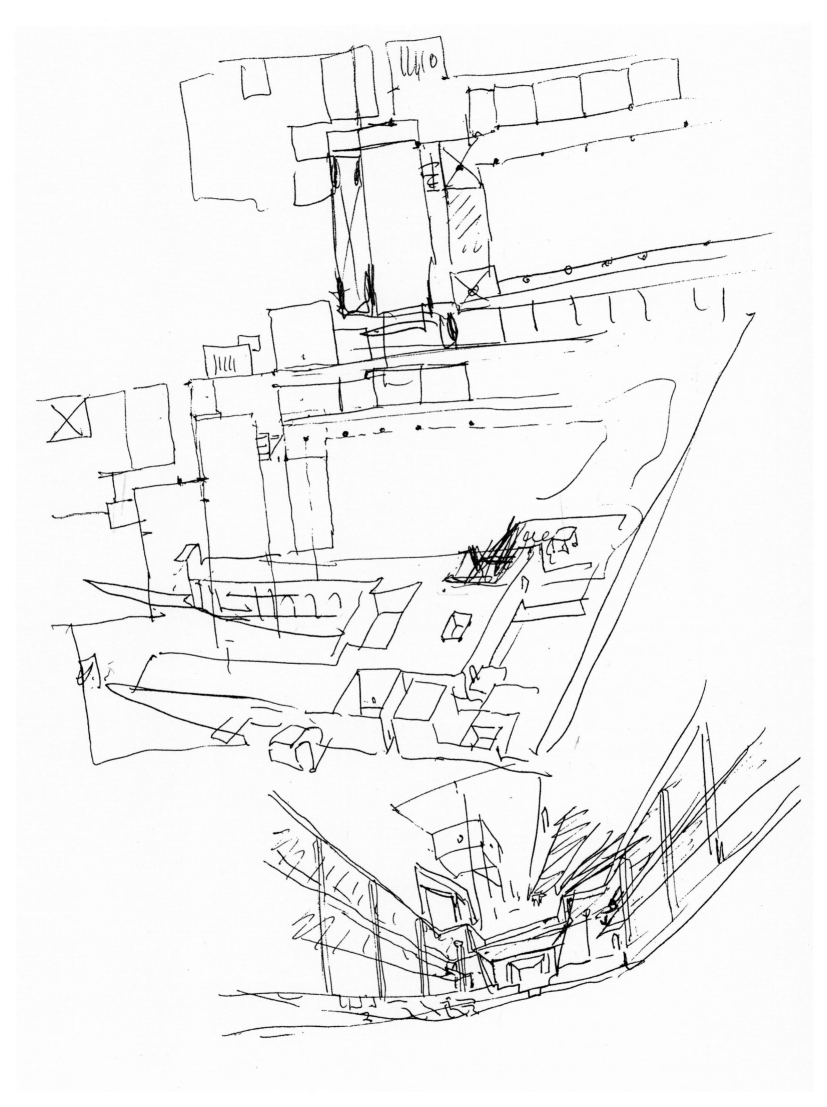

204   Preliminary studies of the floor plan, volumes
and inner courtyard.
205   Short side of the inner courtyard.

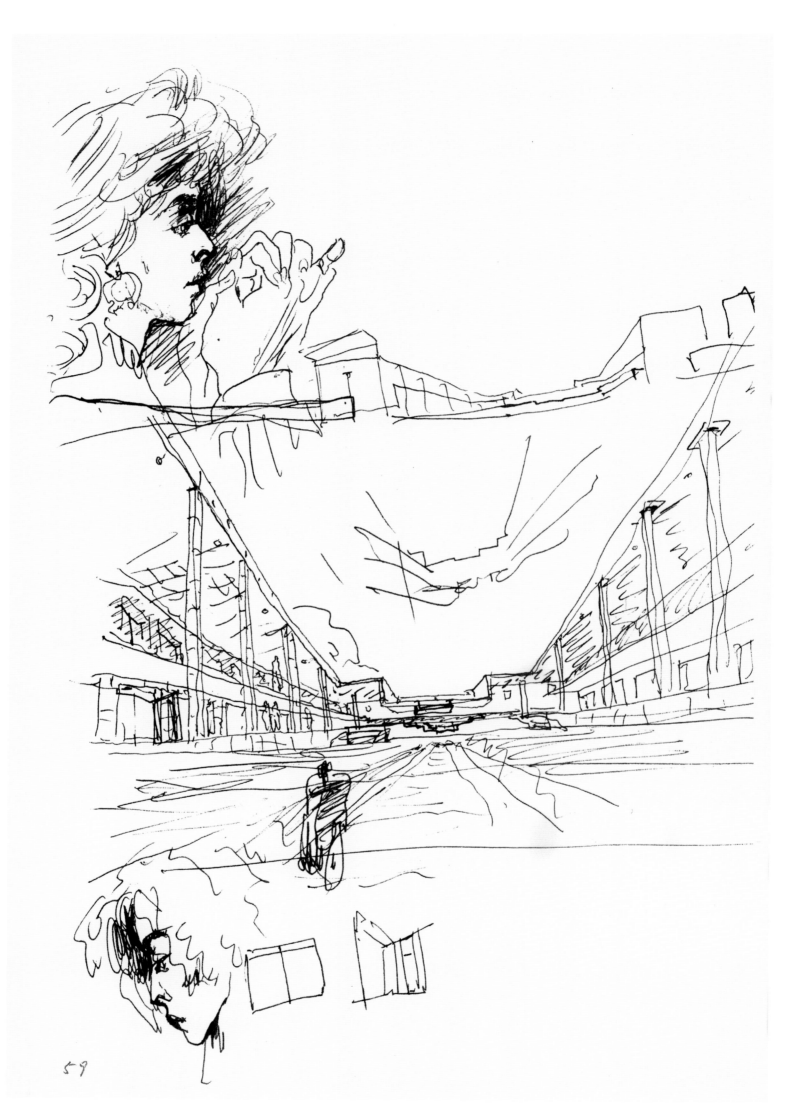

59

206 Sketches of the inner courtyard.
207 Inner courtyard at night with a retained tree
in the foreground.

COLLEGE OF EDUCATION

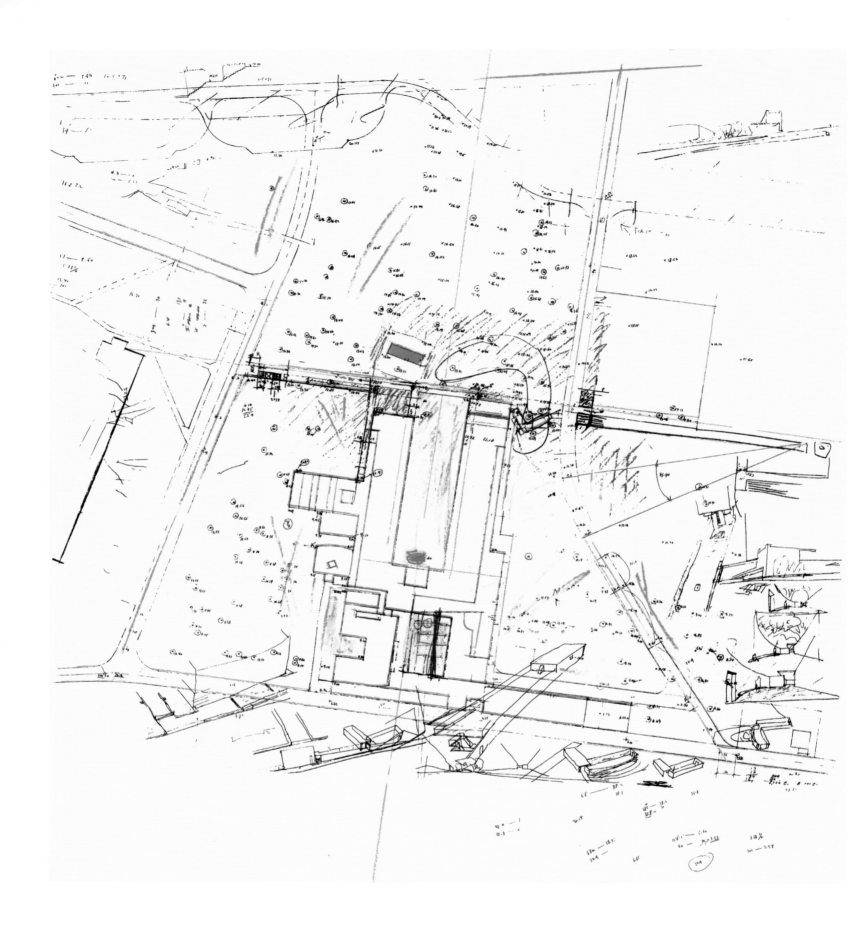

208 Site plan with sketches.
209 The guest house from the porch of the southern
longitudinal volume.

COLLEGE OF EDUCATION

210 and 211   The porch at the end of the southern volume is connected to a side entrance protected by walls painted pink.

COLLEGE OF EDUCATION

212   Main entrance hall.
213   First-floor corridor with a round window overlooking the entrance hall and its rooflight.

COLLEGE OF EDUCATION

214   Library.
215   Top: Main staircase leading to the first floor.
Centre: Gymnasium. Bottom: Main staircase with
cafeteria beyond.

COLLEGE OF EDUCATION

INSEL HOMBROICH
ARCHITECTURE MUSEUM
Neuss, Germany, 1995–2008

Prior to becoming a museum, this design plan was intended to serve a biophysics institute, yet ideas continued to evolve over the next thirteen years, changing the initial programme. Having purchased a former military camp in 1994, the Insel Hombroich Foundation eventually earmarked the land for the construction of pavilions designed by architects from around the world and dedicated to the arts.

As a result, the purpose of this particular building changed, now serving as the architecture museum and photography archive for the Foundation's collection. An informal path leads to the main entrance, and that main entrance immediately reveals the intention of the project. All parts are orientated around a central courtyard, framing the view of the landscape and the distant profile of Düsseldorf. Detached from the main body and supported by an extending wall is a volume dedicated to the photography collection.

The exterior walls are lined with the same irregular brick as the previously constructed buildings of the Foundation, reclaimed from old houses. Oak supports the roof and decks the floor.

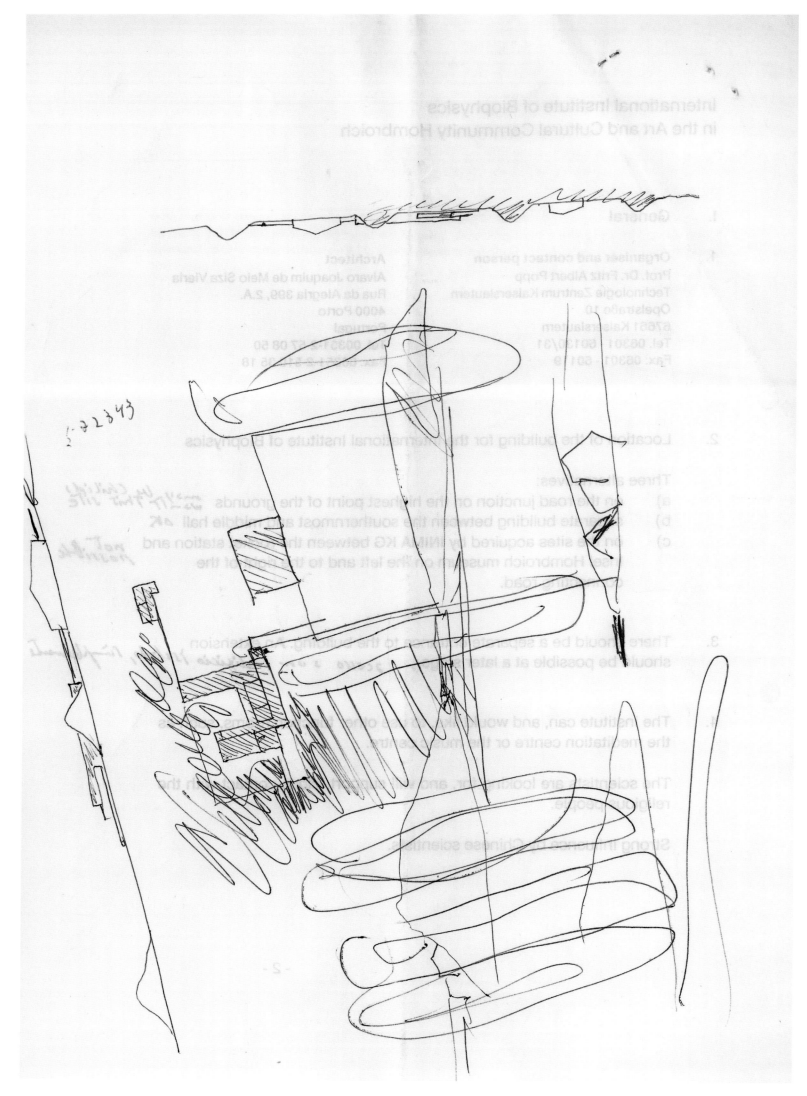

218   Site plan study and schematic sketches
of the elevations.
219   View from the northwest.

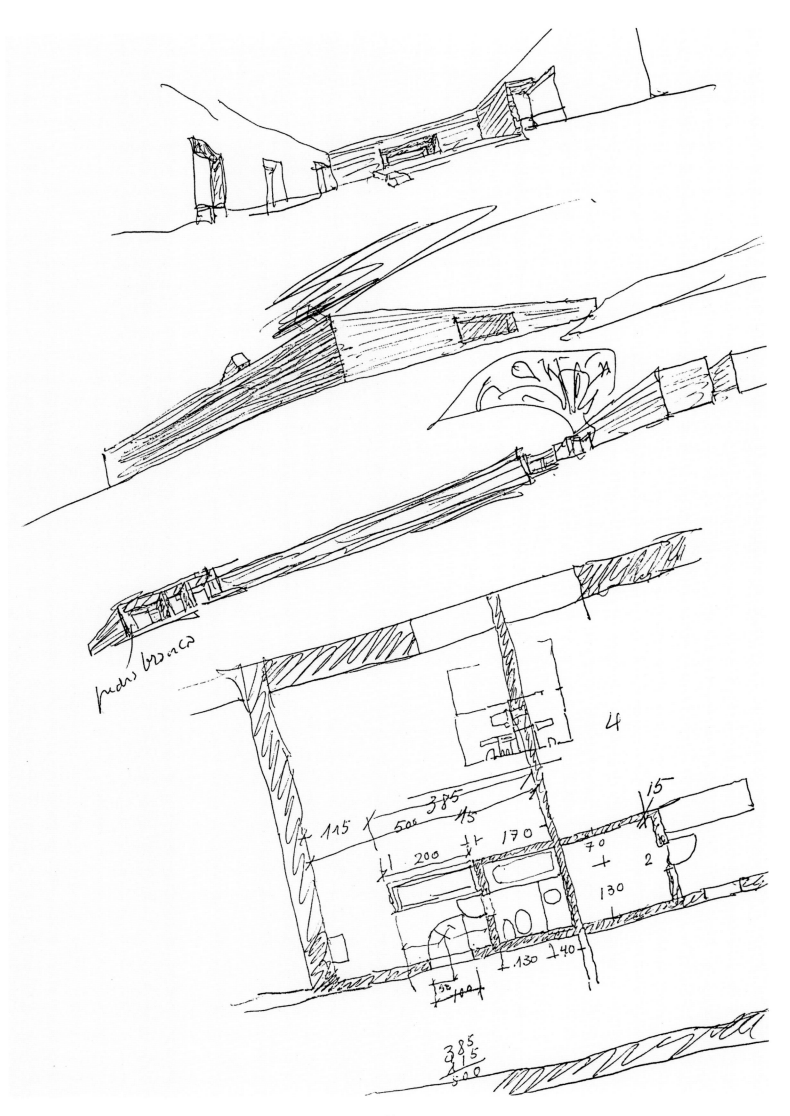

pedra branca

385
15
500

220 Sketches for the patio, south elevation and north elevation, and plan study for the volume containing the photography collection.
221 Top: The courtyard. Centre: Main entrance seen from the northwest. Bottom: West elevation, with the wall connecting the main volume to the photographic collection on the left.

222 Detail of the 'meditation corner' in the west facade.
223 The wall connecting the main volume with the photographic collection building, seen from inside the meditation corner.

224 Studies for the exhibition space.
225 Main exhibition space.

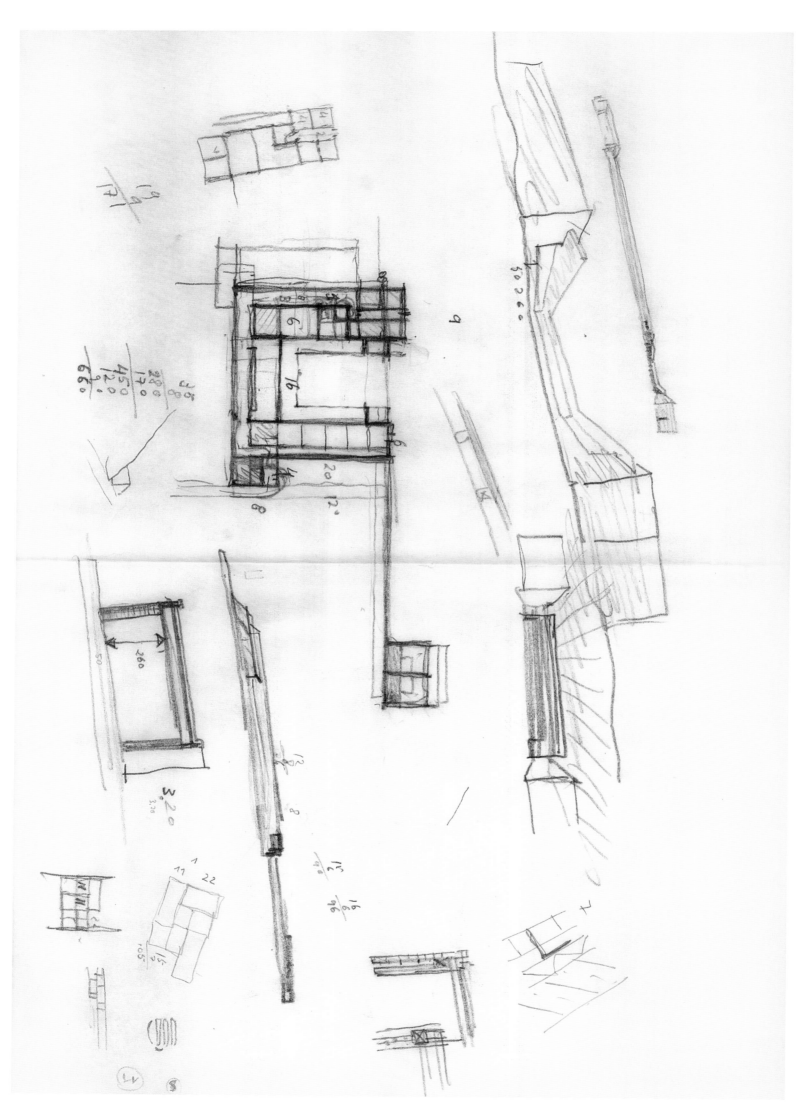

226   Plan study with sketches of different solutions
for the exterior volumes and interior spaces.
227   Interior views of the exhibition spaces.

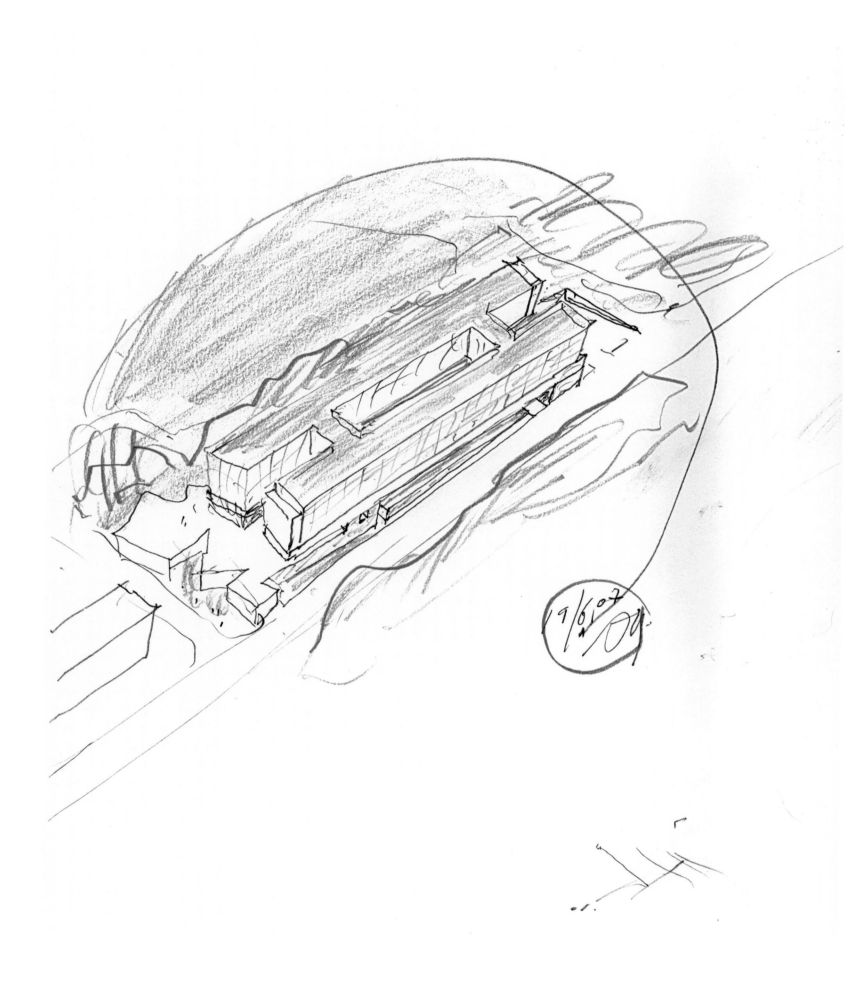

228

AMOREPACIFIC RESEARCH AND DESIGN CENTRE

Yongin-si, South Korea, 2007–2010

Text by Carlos Castanheira, co-author of the project

The studio's first chance to work on a project in South Korea coincided with a visit by the owner of the cosmetic beauty company Amorepacific to Portugal to see works by Álvaro Siza. Knowing the architects who accompanied him, I acted as a guide, with the aim of formalizing an invitation to design a museum in Korea.

The cosmetics company, which had been founded by the present owner's father, began (almost by chance) to collect objects relating to the well-being of women, among them cosmetics, clothing, adornments and items relating to the tea ceremony. Today, the collection is immense, consisting of pieces of national value and interest, as well as great quality and beauty. Enthusiastic, the client wanted to build the museum for this collection in the city centre of Seoul, and to that end, he bought more land — something scarce in those parts and expensive, very expensive. We waited, but the first project did not leave the ground.

A forty-minute drive from central Seoul, on the outskirts of Yongin-Si, Amorepacific has a great property we referred to as 'Campus.' The company's research and development buildings, and training spaces are gathered there. On the site, there is a large structure of grey granite where the various research laboratories are clustered. This building is the result of various additions and adaptations and urgently needed major restructuring.

In another standalone building, this one of dark brick, is the staff training facilities and the improvised museum, displaying only a small part of the collection. The rest — always growing — is stored in the basement.

The outdoor area is characterized by an impressive collection of trees and shrubs the client brought in from elsewhere. In Korea, everything is transplanted, from huge, sculptural pines, like the ones we are used to seeing in the prints of the Far East, to the smallest maples in glowing colours.

At the beginning of the project, we designed the new laboratory to be built beside the existing one, allowing for the relocation of most services and the reuse of old equipment. Given the tight schedule, we then had to consider an additional laboratory building due to the predicted expansion of the campus in the future. And then, why not rethink the surrounding landscape, since by that time the relationship between the existing and projected buildings was so obvious? A campus is just that, a relationship between buildings, where the outdoor spaces act as support. Or is it the other way around?

The laboratory building is big because the programme is big: basement parking; social and technical areas in the semi-basement; two floors of research and workspaces, which look as if they levitate above the ground in order, maintaining the relationship between the space and surrounding views. The social areas include exhibition spaces for the company's art collection, meeting rooms, a restaurant, two conference rooms (one of which is in an amphitheatre) and a health club.

The research floors are as open as possible, as the client expressly wished, certainly influenced by the spaces at the University of Aveiro Library (also by Siza) and according to the necessary safety regulations. The volume that forms the base is clad in slabs of slightly rough black granite. On a partly landscaped terrace below, various paths converge, and the separation of the ground and what is suspended in cantilevers begins. The volume of the laboratories is almost entirely covered with a glazed, double-skin facade over a metal structure. The finishes vary between zinc and white marble stone, differentiating spaces and functions. Despite being a container of so many functions, the building is — through the richness yet simplicity of its materials — turned into a kind of reverse Pandora's box, in which the most beautiful things will originate and help empower the women of Korea.

230   Studies of various solutions for the southern volume.
231   Southern volume seen from the southwest.

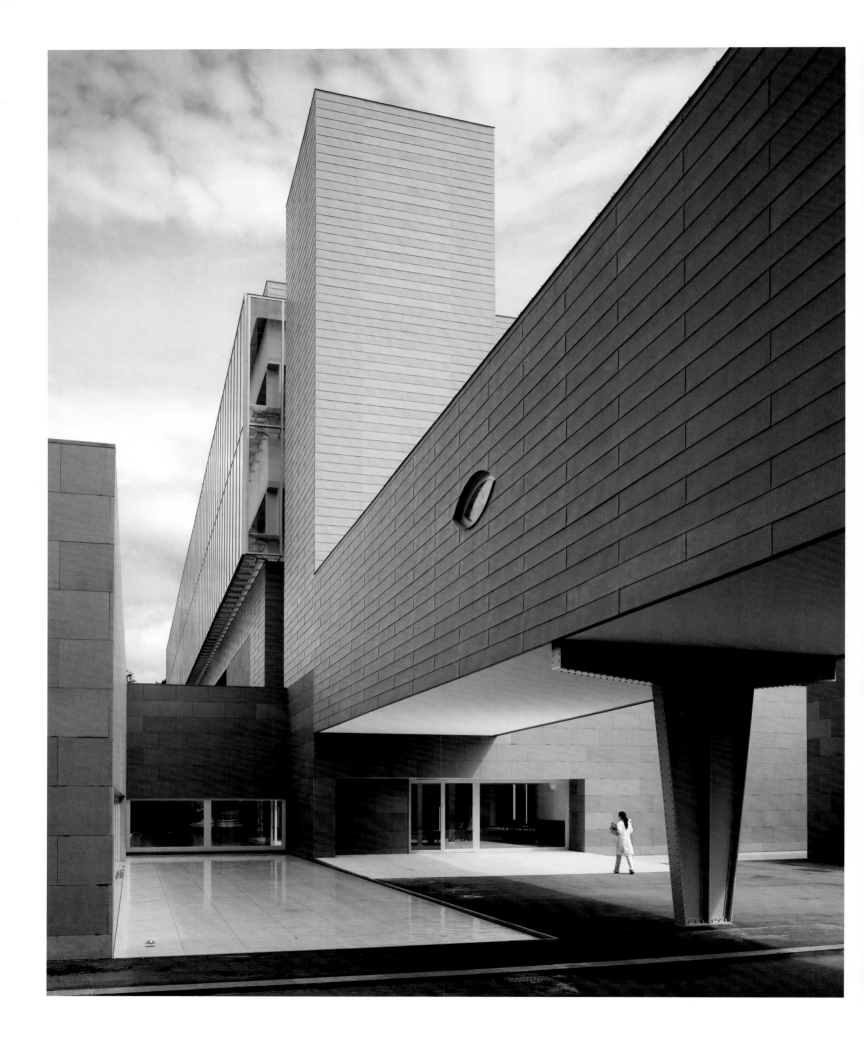

232   Northern volume seen from the west, with the
bridge connection to the older building on the right.
233   West elevation, with entrance courtyard and
connecting bridge on the left.

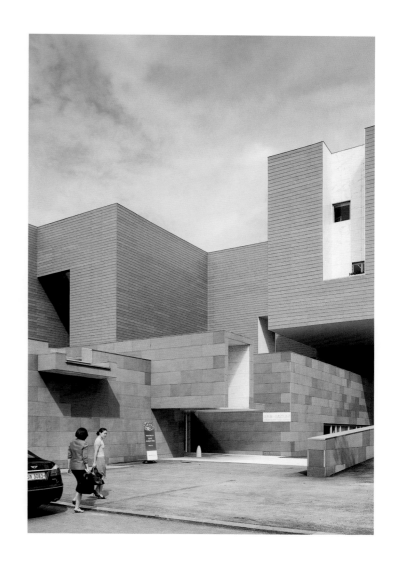

234 Studies for the curtain walls.
235 Top: Side entrance in the southwestern corner of the complex. Bottom: The lobby courtyard at the western end of the complex.

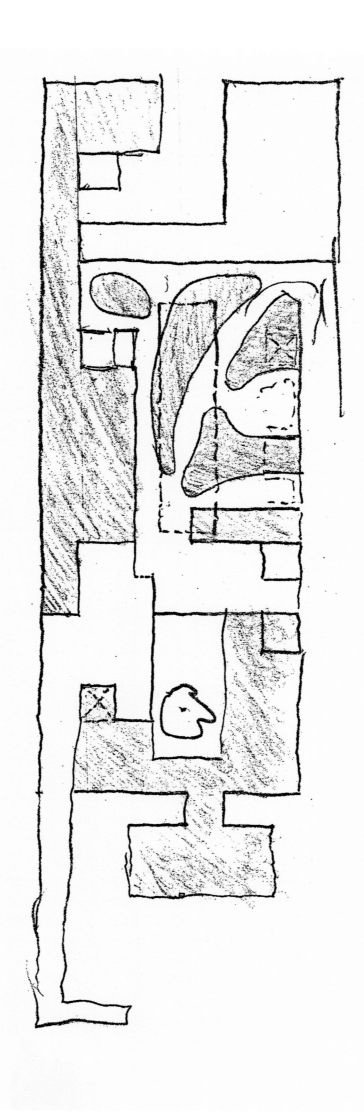

236

236 Concept plan of the complex.
237 The northern and southern volumes seen from
the podium garden.

237   AMOREPACIFIC RESEARCH AND DESIGN CENTRE

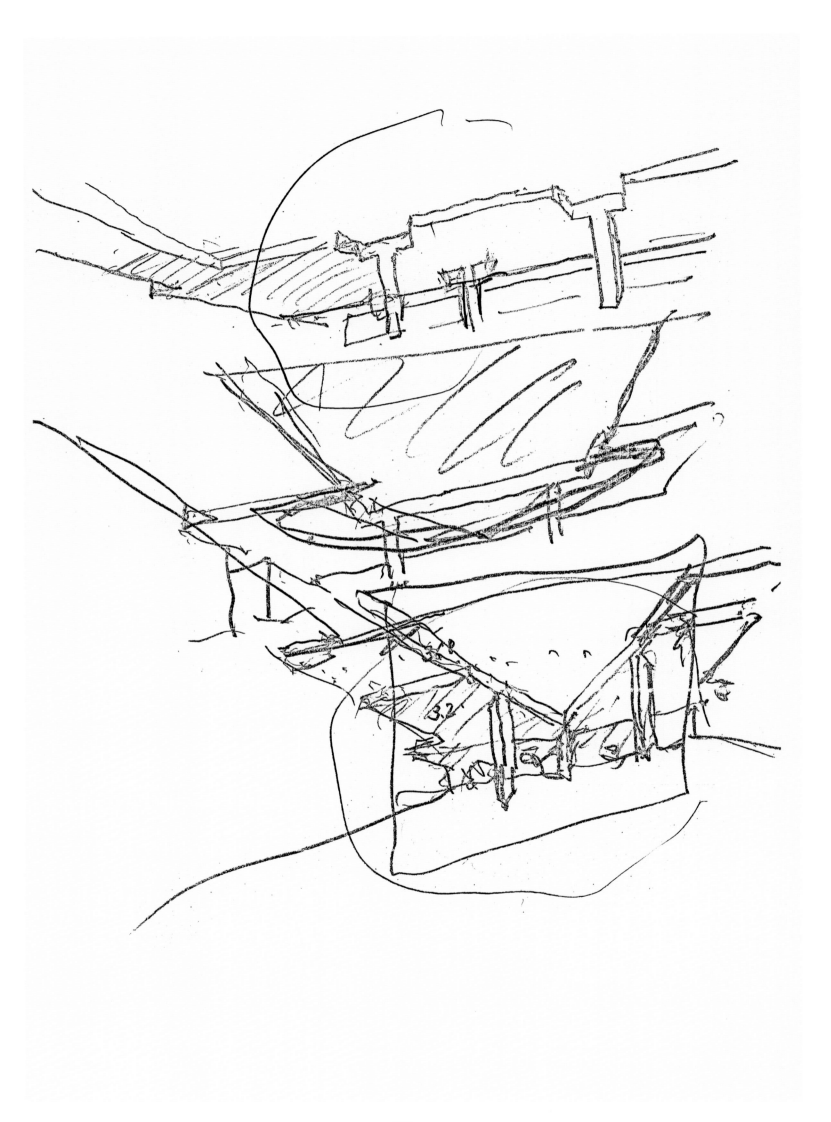

238   Studies for the interior of the lobby and the ground–
floor circulation spaces.
239   Top and Bottom: Circulation spaces on the ground
floor, showing the internal courtyards. Centre: Canteen.

239   AMOREPACIFIC RESEARCH AND DESIGN CENTRE

240   Interior of the bridge connecting the old building
with the new complex.
241   Partial view of the lobby.

15

MIMESIS MUSEUM

Paju Book City, South Korea, 2006–2009

Text by Carlos Castanheira, co-author of the project

A cat has become a museum.

There once was a Chinese emperor who loved cats. One day, he called upon the most famous painter in the empire and asked him to paint him a cat. The artist liked the idea and promised that he would work on it. A year passed, however, and the emperor remembered that the painter still had not given him the painting. He called him and asked: 'What of the cat?' 'It is nearly ready,' answered the artist. Another year went by, and another and another. The scene kept repeating itself. After seven years, the emperor's patience grew thin, and he sent for the painter. 'What of the cat? Seven years have gone by. You have promised and promised, but I still haven't seen one!' The painter seized a sheet of rice paper, an inkwell and one of those brushes that you find only in the East, and, in an elegant and sublime gesture, drew a cat – not just a cat, but the most beautiful cat ever seen. The emperor was ecstatic, overwhelmed with its beauty. The emperor asked the artist how much he would charge for such a beautiful drawing, and the painter requested a sum that surprised him. 'So much money for a drawing you did in two seconds in front of me?' he said. 'Yes, Excellency, that is true, but I have been drawing cats for seven years now,' replied the poor painter.

The design of the Mimesis Museum in the new town of Paju Book City, South Korea, is a cat. The client didn't have to wait seven years for his drawing of a cat, but Álvaro Siza has been drawing cats for more than seven years now.

In one day, I briefed Siza about the plot and showed him a small site model, clarifying the boundaries and the immediate context. In a single gesture, a cat was drawn. The museum is a cat. A cat, all curled up and also open, that stretches and yawns. It's all there. All you need to do is look and look again. At first, the design team could not understand how that sketch of a cat could be a building. I have seen many sketches of cats in my time, and I am always overwhelmed by and never tire of them. I want to see more cats, more sketches of cats, for several times seven years have gone by.

In architecture, after the first sketch comes the torment: the initial design, models, drawings, corrections to these, doubts, new drawings, new models, and finally a presentation to the client, who had already seen other projects but could not conceal his surprise at this one. Once it was approved, the project progressed through the usual steps, which in Korea are shorter and less bureaucratic than in Europe. The brief did not alter, but it was necessary to make adjustments as part of the design's evolution, to think about materials, techniques, infrastructure and representational conventions, so that everyone understood in an attempt for everything to come together.

In the basement, there is an archive as well as an extension to the exhibition area, as is becoming typical in museums designed by Álvaro Siza. The ground floor is a space for arrival and circulation, as well as temporary exhibitions and a cafe. Administration areas are on the mezzanines and the top floor is for exhibitions.

Light, always light, has been so carefully studied. Both natural and artificial light are seen as essential, allowing visitors to see without the source of light being seen. Models and more models were constructed, some of which you could enter, as well as three-dimensional images. The form was given by cast concrete in light grey, the colour of a cat. Inside, the walls and ceilings are white, with marble features, and the timber frames are a honey-coloured oak. As for the external windows, the frames are made of wood and painted steel.

To draw a cat is really difficult – try it! It can take seven years, at least!

242 and 244   Preliminary sketches of the plan and volume.

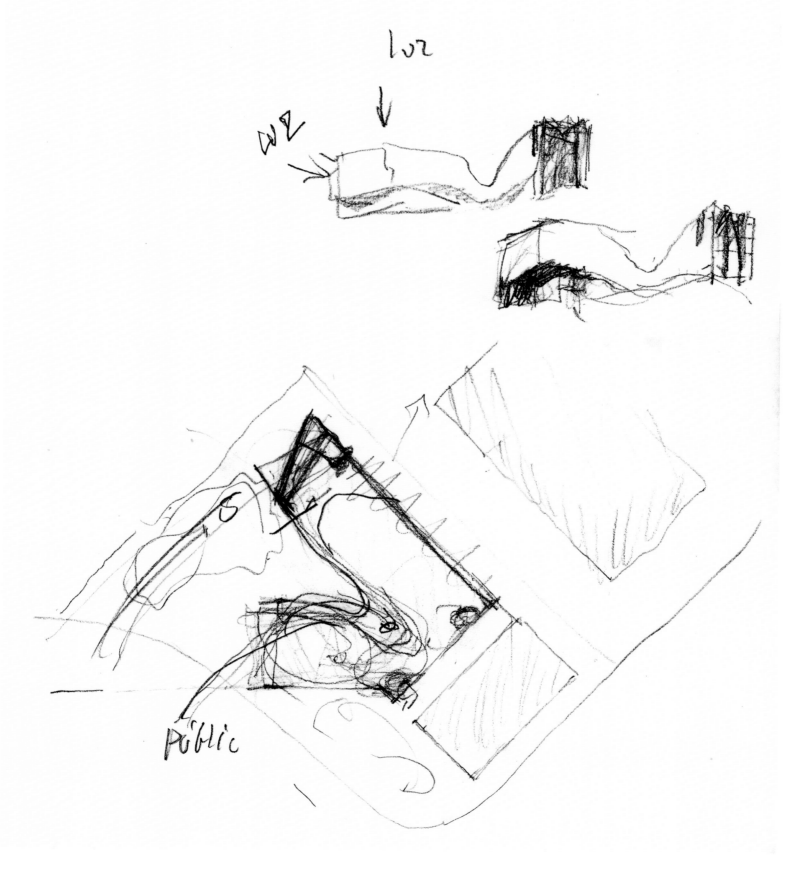

luz

WZ

Public

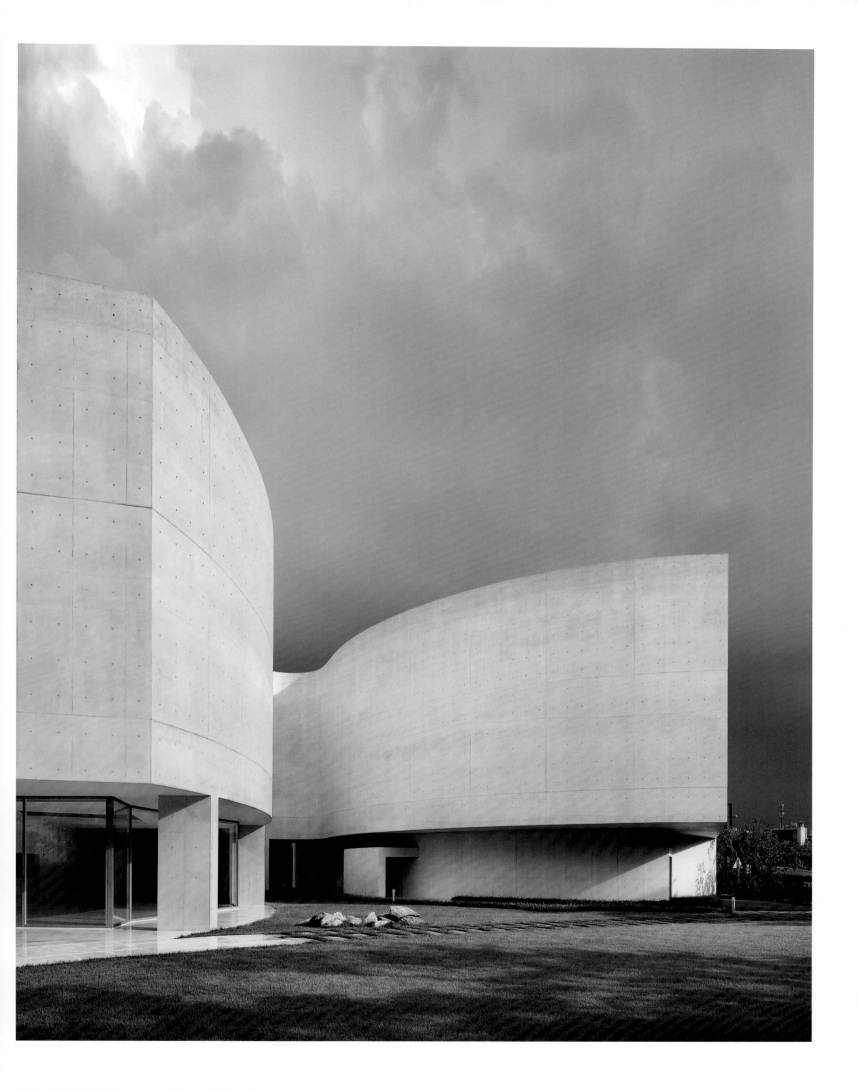

245 and 246   Northwest partial views of the volume,
with the entrance in the centre.

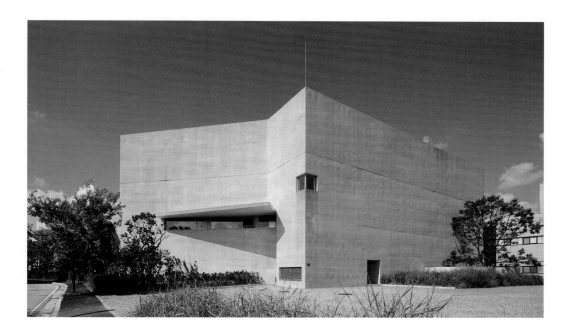

247 Top: Southeast elevation, a view that is now almost completely lost owing to the construction of a new building very close to the museum. Centre: The building seen from the south. Bottom: The building seen from the west.

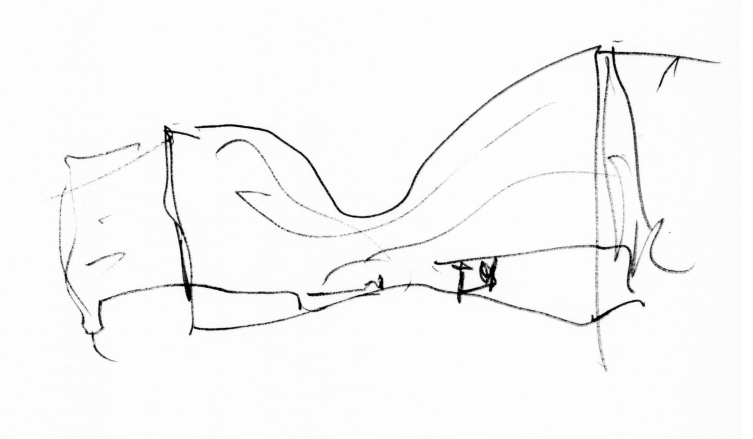

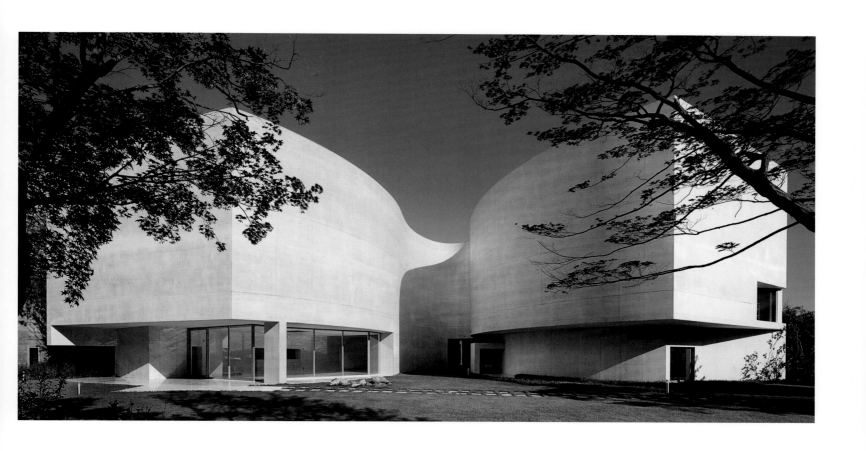

248 Drawing of main volume silhouette.
249 View of museum from the northwest.

250   The sunken courtyard attached to the south facade.
251   Interior of the ground floor close to the entrance,
with a view of the east wing on the right.

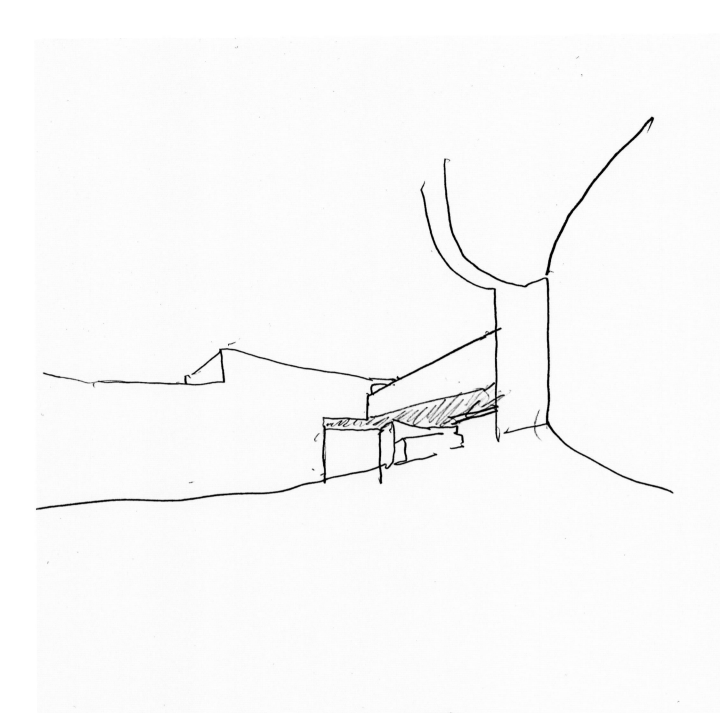

29.7

252   Sketch of the entrance area, seen from the east wing.
253   The entrance area seen from the west wing, showing
the curved staircase that leads to the mezzanine and the
first floor in the background.

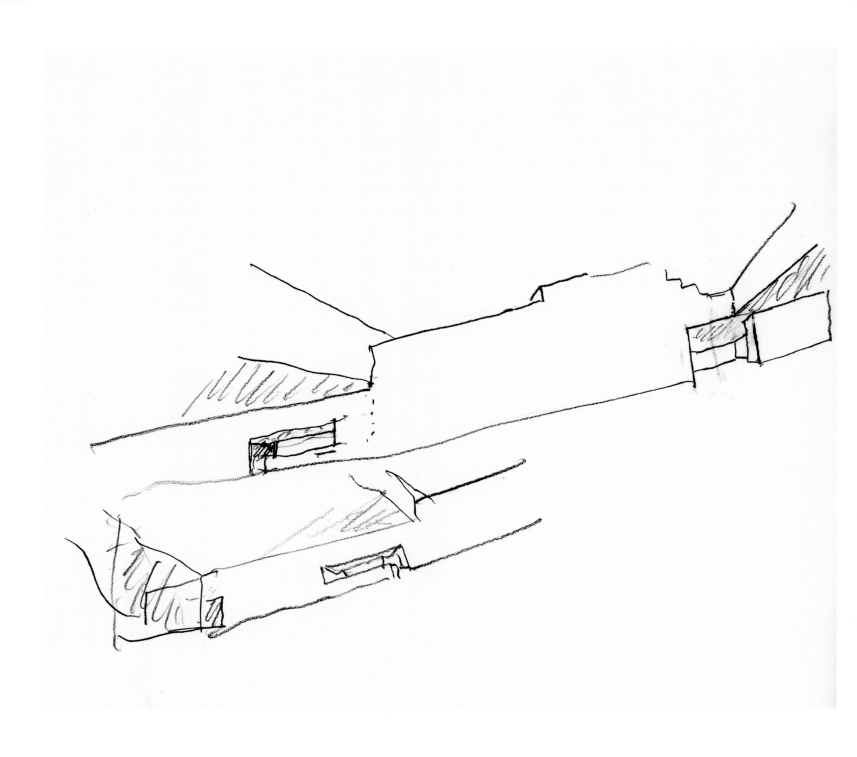

254 Interior sketches.
255 Top: Interior of the first floor of the east wing, with the landing of the access staircase on the left. Centre: Opposite view of the east wing first-floor interior, showing the rooflight that visually connects the ground-floor exhibition spaces. Bottom: Interior of the exhibition spaces on the first floor of the west wing.

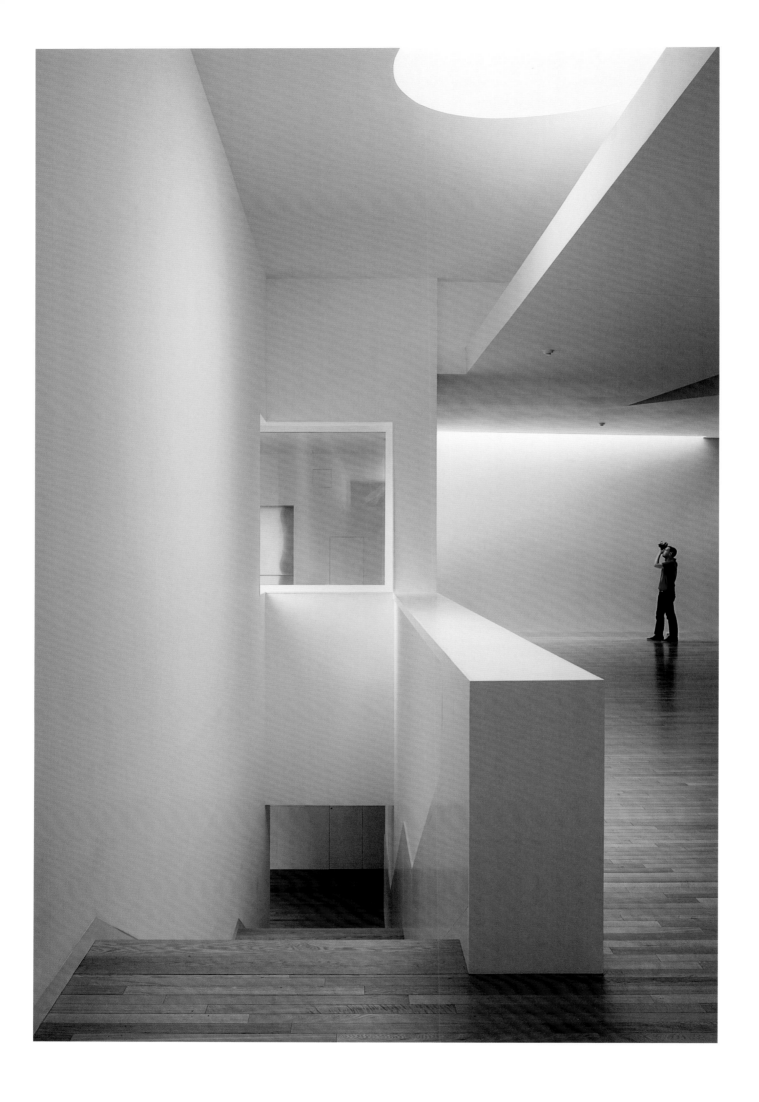

256 Detail of the landing of the staircase that leads to
the exhibition spaces on the first floor.
257 Overview of the exhibition spaces on the first floor.

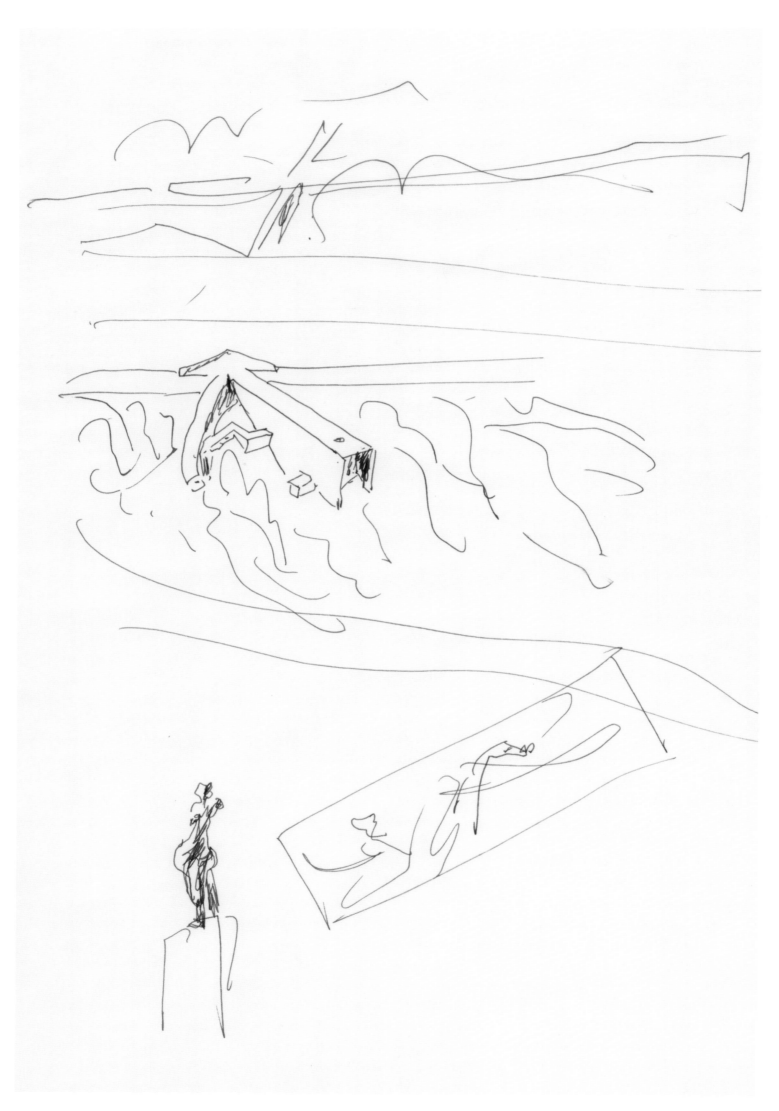

SAYA PARK ART PAVILION

Gyeongsangbuk-do, South Korea, 2015–2018

Text by Carlos Castanheira, co-author of the project

Some projects are born both out of their site and for it, and there are projects that create the site for themselves. The Saya Park Art Pavilion modified the hill site and also adapted itself to it. And we all adapted ourselves to the beauty of the project.

There was a strong inclination to build this particular idea on that site, so all challenges were overcome. The forest path makes its way between high concrete walls, rough in texture but elegant in form. We pass an isolated volume destined for study and information: the library.

We enter the art pavilion as if entering a giant sculpture that absorbs us and enables us to feel space, light, shade, time and what is before and beyond.

Having come to the end of the route, we are presented with an external view of infinity. Inside the space, we look for our own internal, personal infinity.

In architecture space is time.
In architecture light defines form.
In architecture the route surprises.
In architecture rough materials convey elegance.
In architecture the function is being there.
In architecture the shadow reveals the beauty.

258   Sketch belonging to the series 'Visions for Madrid' for an art pavilion to contain *Guernica* (1937) by Pablo Picasso. Commissioned in 1992 by the City of Madrid to celebrate its turn as European Capital of Culture, the project remained a theoretical proposal until the owner of Saya Park decided to build it.

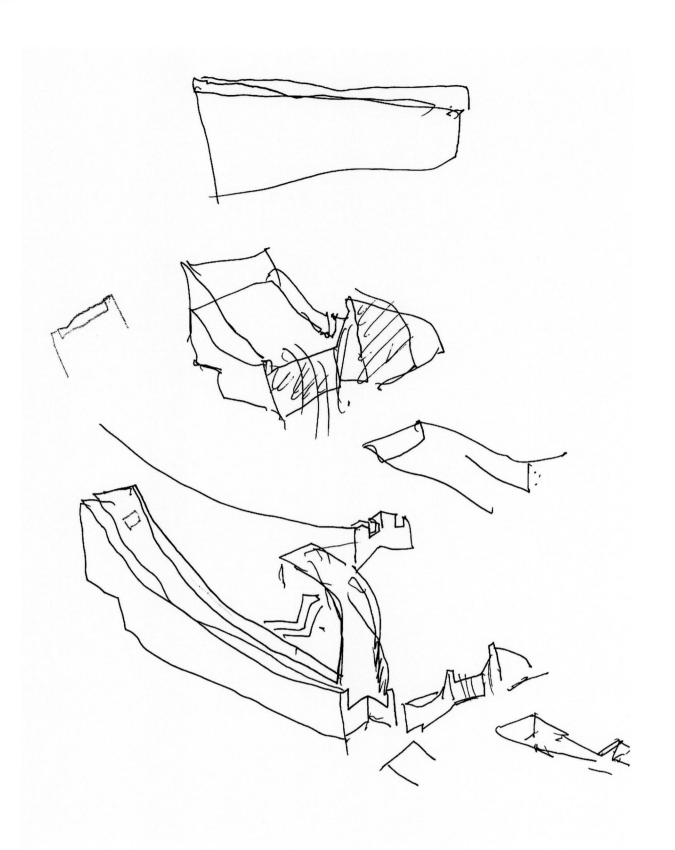

260 Sketch of the art pavilion adapted to the new site.
261 Aerial view from the northeast.

262 Aerial view from the east.
263 Top and Centre: Aerial views from the southeast.
Bottom: View from the roof of the smaller gallery volume.

SAYA PARK ART PAVILION

264   Interior of the smaller gallery volume, looking towards the main entrance.
265   Top: The access courtyard seen from the north.
Centre: The two galleries seen from the main entrance, with the metal pivoting door in the foreground.
Bottom: The inner courtyard.

266   Sketches for the main sculpture, *Untitled* (2017),
designed by Álvaro Siza.
267   Siza's completed sculpture in corten steel,
hanging from a rooflight.

268   Sketches for works of art designed specifically
for this pavilion.
269   The room containing a second sculpture
designed by Siza, *Life* (2017).

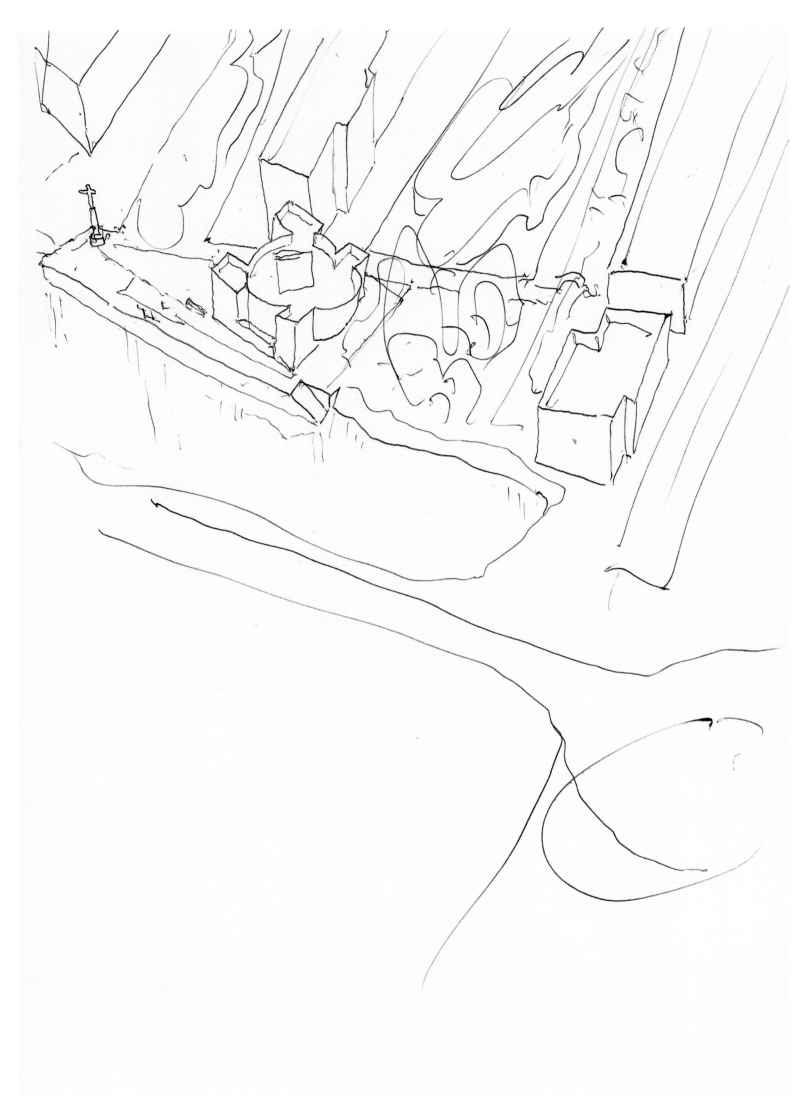

ANASTASIS CHURCH

Saint-Jacques-de-la-Lande, France, 2012–2018

The volumes of this new church for a small town on the outskirts of Rennes were arranged to accommodate the existing street plan and the dimensions of the buildings and spaces nearby, whether built or projected to be built. There was special consideration of the size of the housing complex immediately to the north. Completed in 2022, the new city centre offers 3,000 housing units and a 61-acre park, though the church is considered to be the crown jewel of the project.

As one approaches the church, the bell tower greets them, extending 12.4 meters (41 ft) into the sky. The church is a free-standing building, its programme spread over two floors originating in the superimposition of a cylinder with an outer diameter of 15 meters (48 ft; first floor) and a square of 16 × 16 meters (52½ × 52½ ft; ground floor), with a total height of 12.4 meters. A small basement (97 sq. m / 1,046 sq. ft) houses the technical areas and storage room, and the parish centre and church itself occupy the ground and first floors, respectively. The two floors are connected by two staircases — one of them closed — and a lift.

From this nucleus, and matching it in height, two volumes of rectangular plan extend to the west, framing the atrium that leads to the parish centre and the church. On the eastern side are two similar square volumes, and a cantilevered half-cylinder protrudes from the upper floor.

The parish centre contains a modular room, an office, a kitchen with waste facilities, a reception area and lavatories. The 153.5 sq.-meter (1.652 sq.-ft) central area of the church can seat 126 visitors and is accessible to people with reduced mobility. The south side chapel contains the baptismal font, while the semicircular apse houses the image of the Virgin and the Tabernacle, and the north side chapel accommodates the Cross of Christ. The axis leading from the main staircase towards the crucifix defines the positioning of the altar. The sacristy, with restricted access, is on an upper floor of the volume containing the lift and closed staircase. A raised platform covers the floor of the two chapels as well as the base of the altar and pulpit.

A square platform is suspended above the cylindrical space of the church, controlling the natural light that enters through a roof lantern and containing lighting and ventilation equipment. The sides of this square panel are parallel to the main axis. The church's illumination is thus indirect, adding to the sublime ambience of the holy space. Above the image of the Virgin and the baptismal font are two small lanterns, and the north side chapel is lit by a glazed opening facing west.

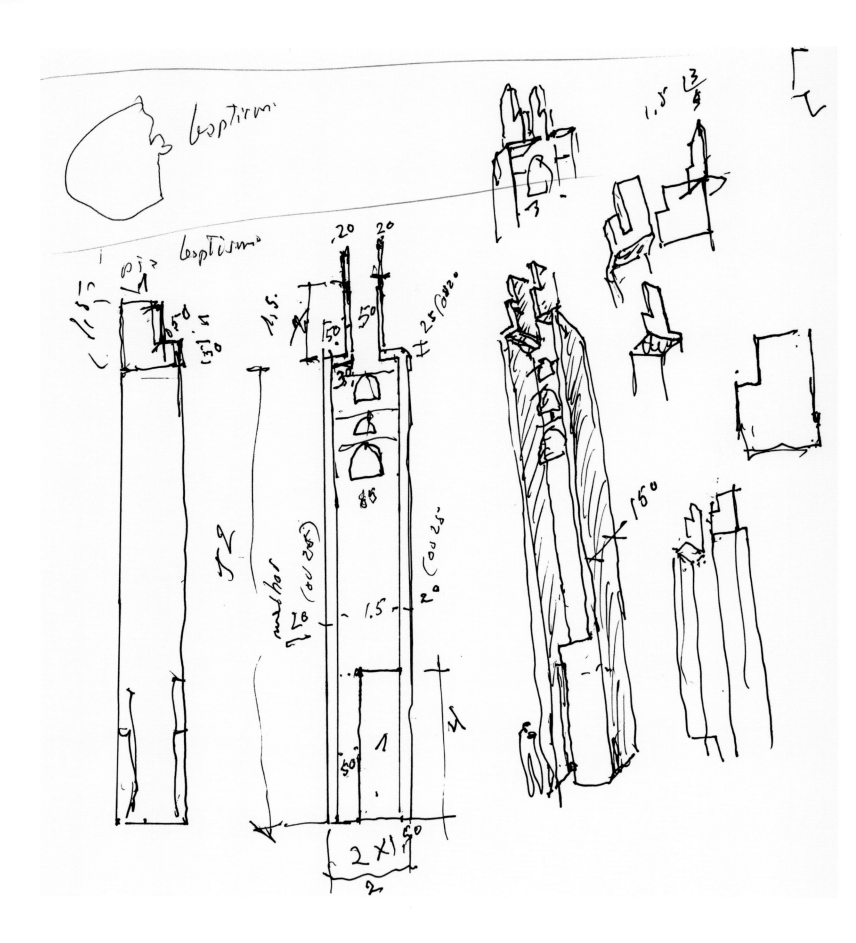

baptism

baptismo

2 x 1.50

272 Studies for the bell tower.
273 The church from the west, with the bell tower
in the foreground.

ANASTASIS CHURCH

274   Preliminary sketch of the church, seen from
the northwest.
275   Top: Main facade of the church, overlooking
the parvis and bell tower. Centre: The southern edge
of the plot is defined by a pool. Bottom: Southeast
view of the church, showing the protruding volume
of the apse.

ANASTASIS CHURCH

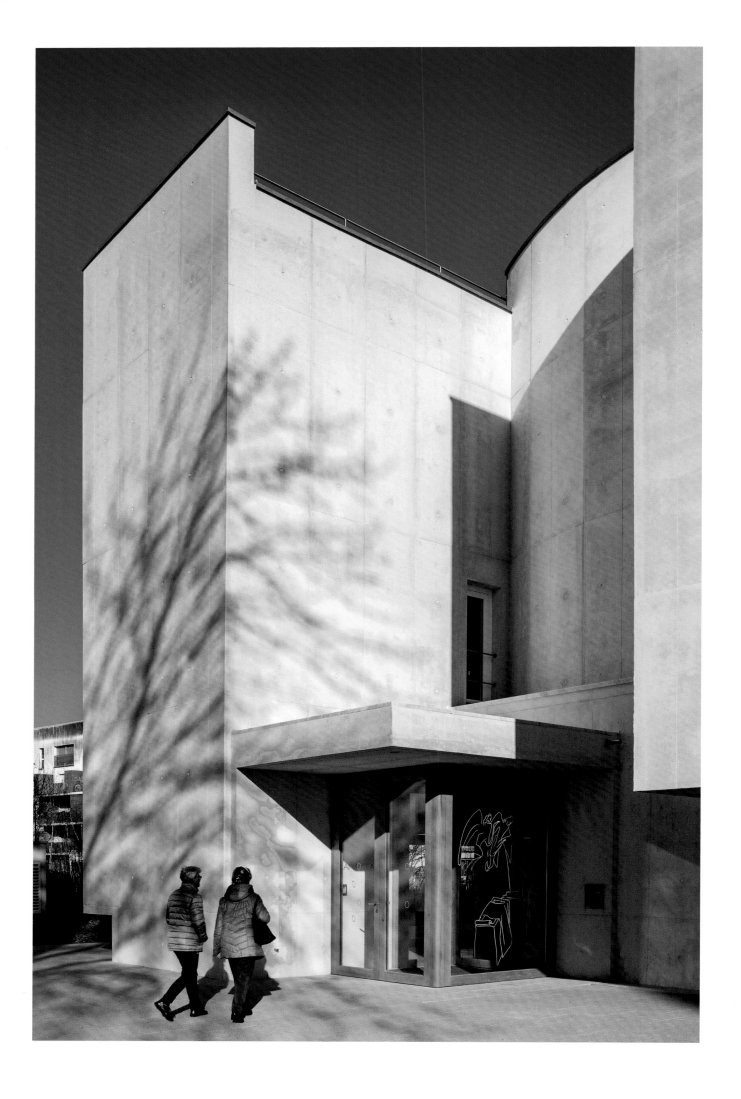

276   Main entrance.
277   Access staircase, with the church space beyond.

ANASTASIS CHURCH

278 Studies for the interior of the church, showing
the altar and suspended ceiling.
279 Side view of the altar.

280   Ceilings, with the wooden crucifix in the foreground.
281   Overview of the interior of the church, with the altar
and wooden crucifix in the background

ANASTASIS CHURCH

282   Sketch study for the baptismal font.
283   Statue of the Virgin, created by Georges Sorraz
in the 1930s, with the font beyond.

OCEAN SWIMMING POOLS
Leça da Palmeira, Portugal, 1961—1966

Every year, with high tides, the sea takes away what is not essential.

At this site, a rocky mass disrupts three parallel lines: the line where sea and sky meet, the line where beach and sea meet, and the line of the large wall that retains the seafront promenade. Someone thought to protect a depression of that massif and use it as a tidal pool.

But the Atlantic Ocean is not the Mediterranean Sea, nor was it simple to build a pool where few are made. Water treatment, demanding regulations and the requirement of approval from several agencies all caused problems.

'The best thing is to call an architect.'

Nothing has changed drastically. The facilities building is anchored like a boat in the wall of the seafront promenade. It won't go anywhere.

Concrete walls support the copper and pine roof as well as access routes to the pool. These paths already existed in the rough terrain (people knew how to choose where to put their feet), the tank of the pool was there, and the walls were parallel to the granite wall of the avenue, from which they hardly stood out. Here and there, small interventions consolidate the natural platforms.

Little has changed.

During the first high tides, the sea took away some of the wall, correcting what was not right. For seven more years, like Jacob, the architect studied the joints, from north to south, where it was difficult to connect the new with the exist-ing. In such a way, the waterfront plan was developed, delivered and paid for. But it was all considered useless. It was probably thought that the architect chose only where to put his own feet and where not to go, fearful of the dangers of rocks and sea.

Someone said: 'Anyone knows where to put his feet, and an architect is sup-posed to put his feet in different places from everybody else.' And then they fired him.

284   Sketch view from the coastal road to the north, with the harbour of Leixões in the background.

285

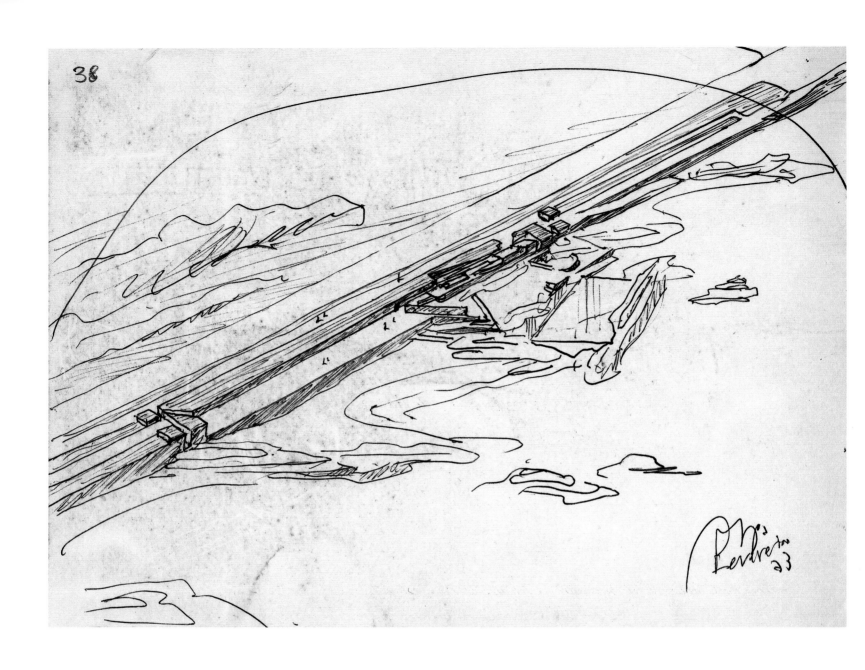

286   Aerial view of the complex from the ocean side.
287   The bar and changing rooms seen from the road,
with the harbour beyond.

OCEAN SWIMMING POOLS

288 Perspective from inside the complex, looking
towards the road.
289 The changing-room volume emerging from
among the rocks and the children's pool.

OCEAN SWIMMING POOLS

290   The pools with the ocean beyond.
291   Top: Lifeguards patrol the small concrete
bridge over the beach of the children's pool.
Centre: The children's pool with the changing rooms
in the background. Bottom: The children's pool with
the ocean and harbour beyond.

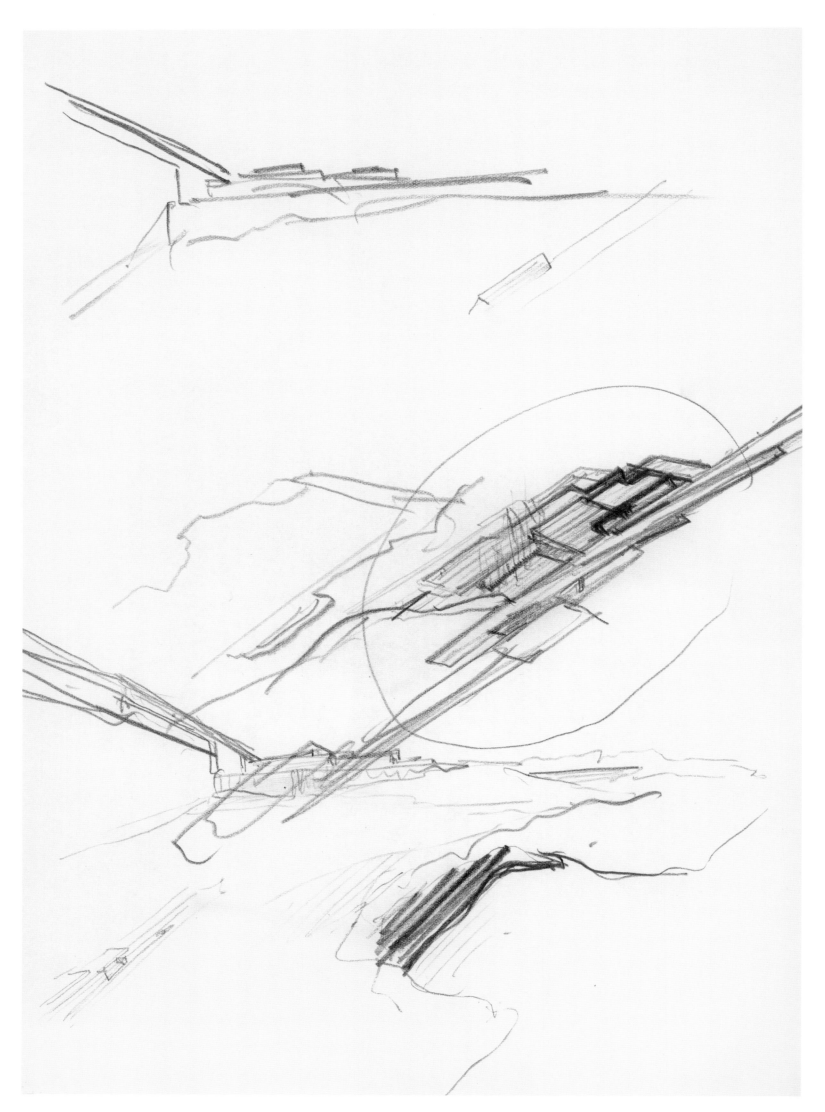

292 Preliminary studies.
293 Walls protect the path between male
and female changing rooms.

294 Interior of changing rooms.
295 Entrance to changing rooms.

OCEAN SWIMMING POOLS

LOOKING BACKWARDS

Álvaro Siza and Duccio Malagamba

Duccio Malagamba: As mentioned in the foreword, the central idea behind this book is to highlight the fascinating — almost magical — connection between the first concepts of the projects and the works as finally carried out. It will be clear to the reader by now that we have done this by juxtaposing the initial sketches with photographs of the finished buildings. We would have liked to follow the same scheme with the text, but no writings are available that reflect the research and ideas in a parallel and contemporary way to the realization of the preliminary sketches.

The texts that accompany the images are, therefore, the project descriptions. These are summaries, generally intended to present the projects, written at various times between the beginning and end of construction, when the projects were almost configured in their final form. For this reason, they must be assigned to the section of our book that we could call 'after'.

As a consequence, the 'before—after' dialectic that is so effective with the images was missing for the texts. That is why we thought of introducing a look at the projects from the present moment. This tour, leafing through the almost finished book, brings out considerations and memories that re-create the spirit of this publishing adventure. Although, strictly speaking, more than a 'before—after', this is an 'after—after' gaze.

Álvaro Siza: When I speak of a project, all my other projects are present, consciously or unconsciously. When I work on a project, it is the same; consciously or unconsciously, all my other projects are present. In the end, architects always work on the same project. With the evolution of their thoughts about architecture, and the information and knowledge that they are acquiring, it is one single job.

Focusing on the various projects presented in this book, we can say that they are projects that I call 'happy' that went well. In fact, they are in the minority, since projects often face obstacles, conflict, and financial or political problems.

In relation to the Santa Maria Church and Parish Centre in Marco de Canaveses, I must thank the parish priest, Don Higino, for backing the project with great commitment. In the ecclesiastical hierarchy, it was not very well understood that the project was commissioned from me, and his support reached the point of threatening to leave the parish in the event that my involvement was rejected. I did not know him before, but I suppose he found out about me through other architects, magazines or books … The fact is, I always had his full support.

It should also be stressed that Don Higino had, with some effort, been able to unite the community around the parish, which received my proposal positively. Perhaps not so much at the beginning, but I made an effort to explain the reasons for certain decisions, and I managed to gradually develop a fairly generalized confidence that, apart from some small difficulties, allowed me to work with ease. Approval by the city council was simple and fast, too — and that is something rare.

The construction process faced financial difficulties because the Church does not pay for the construction of its temples. As a matter of fact, it was achieved mainly through the efforts of the parishioners themselves, who organized fundraising or donated directly. The city council also made a small contribution, and enough was gathered to undertake the first phase of the project, the construction of the church. Years later, the parish centre could also be carried out.

Thinking about this project and its current state, I cannot avoid mentioning something that worries me a lot: the systematic lack of maintenance. Unfortunately, this is not exceptional, and it is true of the vast majority of public works — and also some private ones — since there is a great lack of a culture of preservation in our society.

296   Girl with the Faculty of Information Sciences, Santiago de Compostela in the background.

The complex is currently in bad condition, since there has not been a single maintenance intervention in its entire life. Unfortunately, such interventions are carried out only once the deterioration is dramatic, requiring difficult and costly restoration, as will be the case for these buildings in the near future. This poor condition also highlights another common problem, especially in buildings where craftsmanship played a major role: the poor quality of the construction. In many European countries, Portugal among them, the tradition of artisanal work is being lost, resulting in a decline in quality. In the case of this church, and even more so in the parish centre, there are construction errors that harm the ageing of the complex, as a separate problem from the lack of conservation. These are errors that cannot be attributed to the design; the Faculty of Information Sciences in Santiago de Compostela was built only three years later using exactly the same construction system and is perfectly preserved ...

Part of the responsibility for these drawbacks is undoubtedly attributable to lax auditing. Nowadays, quality control is usually entrusted to external contractors — instead of the architect who designed the project — and these contractors are not very involved, so in many cases, the inspection is not adequate. This is why buildings with the same construction system sometimes behave well and sometimes badly.

So, in the case of this project, when I look back I cannot forget these construction problems and the unsatisfactory performance of the work over time. Of course, if I had known what was going to happen, I would probably have chosen other construction solutions. Now we will see if — with the restoration that we will have to undertake soon, and which will have to be profound as far as the exterior is concerned — I will be able to reconcile myself to these aspects of the project.

Slightly older is CGAC, the Galician Centre of Contemporary Art in Santiago de Compostela. This project was very important for me because it helped to rescue me from certain marginalization relating to my political past and my experience designing public housing through the SAAL movement. Although, it must be said that, especially in Europe — perhaps also due to the favourable political climate — the process of SAAL was highly valued and publicized, and that gave me the possibility of working outside of Portugal, in Germany and in the Netherlands. But these were always housing commissions because of that deep-rooted belief that divides architects into specialists in this or that. And [after SAAL], I was considered an expert in 'collaborative social housing', a horrible label.

It was essential for me to work with other scales and other types of buildings, in particular public buildings. So CGAC was my first museum, and I am very grateful for the commission from Xerardo Estévez, then mayor of Santiago. Estévez was an architect, but a very special one — he had devoted himself to the study of the city and was not interested in directly designing the projects. In fact, during his time as mayor, he commissioned projects from many well-known national and international architects, and he dedicated himself to following and supporting their work. He did a fantastic job of ensuring the city's recovery and also welcoming the contribution of students and teachers. In fact, his method had certain points in common with SAAL, but of course in an atmosphere of stability and not of revolutionary effervescence, as in the Portuguese case.

The project went well. Needless to say, there were some difficulties during the process, but it was essentially a positive experience, thanks to the support of the mayor and the president of the Galician Autonomous Government, Manuel Fraga Iribarne. Although the two men belonged to opposing parties, there was understanding between them. Both were people of dialogue and despite his previous implication in General Franco's regime, Fraga was an intelligent man.

As I have said, the Faculty of Information Sciences at the University of Santiago de Compostela uses the same construction system as the Marco de Canaveses intervention: large wall sections made up of structural concrete panels, finished with plaster on the outside and with thermal insulation on the inside, with a second plasterboard wall. A school building, a faculty, always has a very interesting programme, because it has rich and varied spaces. It has a library, a large access atrium, spaces for teachers and students to meet, studios and classrooms ...

The articulation of these different areas is what shapes the character of the building — a character that, in this case, is also indebted to the environment, since the building is set in a garden that is part of a university campus. The various buildings that compose that campus were born from an overarching plan into which I could integrate when I built the faculty.

DM: Following our focus on 'before—after', I was wondering if, with the time that has elapsed and the experience you have accumulated, there would be anything you would like to modify in the projects we are analysing. We have seen that in the case of the Marco de Canaveses project, you would like to alter certain technical aspects, but I am curious to know if there is anything in the field of design that you would like to be able to vary …

AS: In relation to design, it is difficult to think about changing something, since the project has a coherence that derives from the technical choices but even more from the 'human environment' at that time. That is why, remembering how that process was, I do not feel the need to change anything. It was something that came naturally out of a certain context, from certain difficulties, from certain demands … I cannot imagine what would have happened in different circumstances.

To clarify what I mean, I can relay what happened when I was commissioned to restore the Casa de Chá Boa Nova teahouse and restaurant [in Leça da Palmeira, near Porto], a project of mine from 1958 that was completed in 1962. I had designed it when I was very young, together with other colleagues, and over time, I had developed a certain self-criticism regarding its relationship with the landscape. I became convinced that we had exaggerated the parallelism between the profile of the landscape and the profile of the building.

So, when I went to inspect the Casa de Chá Boa Nova to undertake its rehabilitation, I was already going with a certain critical spirit. During the visit, I began to notice things that did not convince me, for example, some wooden elements that hung from the ceiling. At first, I thought about eliminating them, but during the visit, I realized that if I changed that detail, I would also have to modify another one, then another one that in some way related to the previous ones … By the end of the visit, I had come to the conclusion that there were only two options: demolish everything or leave it as it was.

The decision not to modify anything gained strength when I realized that if, by modifying one element, I felt the need to modify another and then another, it meant that — at least from my point of view — the project was coherent. And I have not regretted the decision to restore it as it was designed at the time.

The Serralves Museum of Contemporary Art in Porto is another 'happy' project. First of all, it is set in a magnificent garden. This, however, does not belong to the original garden of the Serralves house, and this prompts me to mention a small controversy that originated at the time of construction. There was a current of opinion considering that the construction of the museum would damage the integrity of the historic garden. In reality, the garden was made up of three areas: a forest, an agricultural area and the garden around the Art Deco villa. Created by a French landscaper, Jacques Gréber, who had worked extensively in the United States, the garden manages to combine Art Deco taste with a neo-classical concept.

The new museum was to be built in the area destined for agriculture, and its detractors argued that this would destroy the original continuity. That was false, because the orchard had been recently acquired and had nothing to do with the Serralves garden. Fortunately, this difficulty could be solved fairly easily by consulting historical documents. In fact, one of the concerns of the project was to integrate the new museum garden into the existing garden. In addition, a new path was laid in order to connect and engage the various parts of the estate.

Construction went smoothly and in a very pleasant manner. It was the second museum I had designed, after CGAC, and I was able to take advantage of the experience I had gained in Santiago, especially since both were contemporary art museums. It gives me great satisfaction to see that it works well and is well cared for.

DM: That's also something that contributes to a project becoming a happy project, isn't it?

AS: Of course! As architects, we can no longer accompany our projects when we finish them, but while we are alive, we suffer from seeing our buildings mistreated or misused.

DM: And so we arrive at Granada ... Before I forget, I have to ask you about a sketch in the book (page 82), where you mention [Federico] García Lorca. What does he have to do with the Zaida project?

AS: Here it is: 'García Lorca in my restaurant'. Thinking about Andalusia, it is impossible not to think about Lorca, a fascinating character. I had just reread an anthology of his poems when I was designing the Zaida Building and Courtyard House in Granada, and I couldn't resist evoking the poet. So, in this sketch, I invite him to a virtual restaurant on the roof terrace of my building so that we can contemplate together the magnificent palace of the Rodríguez-Acosta Foundation and its gardens, which are right in front of it. A joke, nothing more ...

In this project, I collaborated with the Granada architect Juan Domingo Santos, with whom I also worked years later on the project for a new entrance and visitor centre at the Alhambra. That was indeed a deeply unhappy project ... We won the international competition, advanced quite far into the design process, and there seemed to be a serious will to carry it out, but then everything stopped!

DM: Well, episodes like the 'reincarnation' of the conceptual project 'Visions for Madrid' into the Saya Park Art Pavilion show that you never know. Maybe a new mayor will take up the Alhambra project and build it ...

AS: I have no hope that it will be reactivated, since it seems that the opposition comes mainly from architects for reasons that are not difficult to discern. Better to change the subject. Let's talk instead about the Family House in Sintra, another building that we can include in our list of happy projects. Once again, the site should be mentioned as a highlight. There, we could count on a splendid plot sloping towards the sea, with the river, the coast ...

The client had very clear ideas about certain aspects of the work. For example, he was very insistent on the concept of 'individual privacy' as well as 'community'. He wanted the spaces in the house to be independent while still belonging to a whole. So, in the end, each room is practically a separate piece, while all are connected by an articulated corridor that acts as a spine. Another of his wishes was that the house should be clad in wood, a proposal that pleased me and that I incorporated into the design. Therefore, we can say that, in this case, there was a positive and enriching exchange of ideas between architect and client.

The Summer House in Majorca has in common with the Sintra house the client's interest in ensuring that the building offered autonomy — in this case, to their grown sons — without losing the sense of being a family home. And, as in Sintra, this is reflected in the design, although in a different way.

The two interventions also share the type of location — privileged plots facing the sea — although the Majorca site was even more spectacular and exclusive, with direct access to the sea and an extraordinary panorama of the island's coastline.

Apart from the fixed furniture that I designed along with the rest of the project, much of the furniture was chosen by the owners themselves, in consultation with me, or selected by designer and architect Fernando Amat. The relationship was very good, and the result has been very good, too.

The Mayor Winery in Campo Maior can also be included in the list of happy projects, mainly because the owner wanted a high-quality work. He didn't discuss small details ... he wanted something well done. Furthermore, he was the owner of a huge property, and that allowed me to choose a very suitable location on a gentle hill in the middle of Alentejo's undulating landscape. In the place I selected, there was a dug-out waste dump, so that cavity was used for the cellar. There were no buildings around it, and during construction, vines were planted in the surrounding fields. It was a landscape of incredible beauty, and it would have been unforgivable not to design a beautiful building. From a landscaping point of view, it was a unique experience to be able to integrate my building into an endless landscape of vineyards and cultivated fields.

I usually say that the client is the first architect, because if the owner is looking for quality, we can achieve it, but if he or she is not interested, it is very difficult to get it. As I have already mentioned, the commitment of the client was very important in Campo Maior, too. For example, it allowed us to include a shallow pool of water in that magnificent roof garden that dominates the landscape and serves as a point of arrival for organized visits to the winery. This pool, while contributing only marginally to the thermal control of the cellar, constitutes an important reference because it introduces water into an environment that is dry for much of the year.

If we focus on the outcome, the SAAL Bouça Social Housing complex in Porto cannot be defined as unhappy, but it was certainly the result of an extremely complicated process. After part of the project was completed, construction was stopped for more than thirty years and the houses were occupied without being finished, causing serious degradation of the complex. During the interruption, the project was spoken of as badly as possible, cited as an example of the incompetence of the architects of the revolutionary period and proof of the ineptitude of the political left. To a certain extent, one can understand the ease with which this criticism was spread: since only a small part of the complex had been carried out, the plan was hardly comprehensible at that time.

Finally, the city council decided to finish the project. The construction was resumed without the inhabitants leaving, despite the poor conditions in which they lived. It was a great satisfaction for me to see the whole complex finished after so much criticism and tribulation. By the way, at that point it was appreciated and praised — in part by the people who had previously denigrated it … but that is also common.

In any case, architectural quality should not be confused with the quality of construction. These are very cheap buildings that require constant preservation. And unfortunately here, too, the effects of that widespread habit of lack of maintenance are beginning to show. In this regard, I can think of a sadly funny episode that happened a few years ago. The cooperative that manages the Bouça homes called me to ask my opinion about the city council's idea to pay a well-known graffiti artist to paint a huge mural — 'the authentic expression of popular art' — there. I replied that if the council had money to spend, it would have been much more urgent to repaint the buildings. The result was no paint and no graffiti! There are some things that are difficult to accept or understand …

The Ribera Serrallo sports complex in Cornellà de Llobregat had a very interesting programme with a sports hall and a large swimming pool — a building of a considerable scale with an inspiring variety of uses. We can consider it an 'almost' happy project because the end was difficult. There began to be a shortage of funds to finish the work well. The realization of the large dome over the pool was complicated, and there had to be a lot of negotiation to correct the failures that occurred there. Looking at the project with some distance, however, the overall balance is positive.

The VMD house and art gallery in Oudenburg, on the other hand, was a happy project without any need for nuance. The family of one of the clients had a farm with some agricultural buildings. It is in a completely flat area of Belgium, crisscrossed by canals — the one sung about by Jacques Brel …

The project consisted of restoring the existing structures and adding an extension so that they could be used for housing. The refurbishment aimed to respect the spirit of the old buildings and their relationship with the landscape. The complex includes a small art gallery because the owner also works as an art dealer and has a good collection of paintings and sculptures. This was another case in which the client was the first architect …

I am beginning to think that in this selection of projects, consciously or unconsciously, we censored the 'bumps in the road' of my professional career, since the public library in Viana do Castelo is another happy project. It is a piece of the plan that the architect Fernando Távora designed to order the riverfront of the city. Eduardo Souto de Moura also participated, designing a multipurpose pavilion next to the library.

At that time, Távora had his studio in the same building that Souto and I still share in Porto. In his office, there was a huge model, and we worked together, discussing how to characterize the buildings while respecting the lines of the riverside development plan. It was a very interesting collaborative exercise: three people who had known one another and shared ideas for a long time, working together … Furthermore, the project was very well received by the city council, and we felt supported. We must not forget, either, that the library is a genre that I really like to design. It is historically a very rich typology, and I had already worked on it with Aveiro University Library (1988–95) and, on a smaller scale, the library for Porto University's faculty of architecture (1986–96).

This is becoming monotonous, because the Iberê Camargo Foundation in Porto Alegre was not just a happy project; it was a very happy project and an unexpected opportunity for me. I received an invitation to enter the competition because one of the people responsible for the process knew and appreciated my buildings. He was José Luiz Canal, an engineer who had studied in Barcelona and surely played an active role in the jury's decision. I also received a very strong endorsement from Dona Maria, the painter Camargo's widow, who, after seeing the model of my project, did not want to see any other. Last but not least, substantial support also came from the main sponsor of the project, Jorge Gerdau, a prominent Brazilian businessman.

Canal was very supportive during construction in terms of team management. His decision not to put the work out to tender was fundamental. Instead, he chose the best craftspeople and the best contractors and formed a team that he directed until the museum was completed. There was excellent collaboration between him, the structural engineer (Jorge Silva) and me. Sometimes, Canal came to Porto, sometimes we went there … at that time, I was in better shape than I am now, and I travelled to Brazil quite a few times.

I am also satisfied with the result of the College of Education in Setúbal, but it was a very long process, and many difficulties of various kinds had to be faced, including approval by the School Services. On the other hand, there was strong support from the management of the school, and thanks to that, we managed to finish well.

Unusually, there I was asked to design all the furniture as well. This is, unfortunately, something that is generally very difficult to achieve, and I am extremely sorry about that. The normal situation is that decorators and interior designers come into play … that is why I wrote 'Interior—Exterior: A Single Design' for this book (page 7).

Today, specialization is in vogue. I was recently excluded from a competition for a health building because I have never built a hospital. This way of thinking makes me desperate; I even wrote a letter to the organizers telling them that the most beautiful hospital I had ever seen was Alvar Aalto's sanatorium in Paimio [Finland], and he had never made a hospital before. This approach is the result of the same culture that considers that the interior and exterior of a building have no relation to each other and that it is acceptable for them to be designed by two different people. [The early twentieth-century architect and theorist] Adolf Loos, for whom such complementarity was the basis of any project, would fall into an existential crisis … This current sad idea can be added to the lack of recognition of the status of the author, the absence of rules for the protection of the profession, the decrease in respect for professional fees …

The Insel Hombroich Architecture Museum is another building that I am quite satisfied with, although it was also slow. It was intended as a biophysics laboratory to house a very sophisticated American-made X-ray apparatus. There were only two or three such machines in Europe. However, problems arose, and the project was stopped. It was later resumed, with the building converted into an exhibition gallery and a small photographic archive.

The environment is very interesting there: an artistic ensemble created by a former construction businessman who, once he had made his fortune, stopped working to dedicate himself to this initiative. The owner of an extraordinary art collection, he built a series of pavilions to exhibit it. Within a large park, which was later extended into an adjacent abandoned NATO missile station, the first pavilions were commissioned from the local artist Erwin Heerich (1922–2004), and they are very, very beautiful. Others were added later, including one by Tadao Ando (1941–) and another by Raimund Abraham (1933–2010).

DM: Let's jump to the Far East now.

AS: To get an idea of how well and how easily the projects in Korea turned out, it is enough to take a look at the construction dates. These buildings in the Far East took an average of three or four years to be completed, including both project and construction times. These are private projects but intended for public or semi-public use. They were quick because they had supportive clients: people really interested in architecture, with great enthusiasm who seek out quality. If we compare it with Europe, I have gruelling projects that have lasted thirteen or fourteen years. Not to mention [the residential project in] Venice, which has been in progress for forty years now and it is still not finished. I believe that is a world record! Excess bureaucracy and the influence of politics have a good deal of responsibility for this situation...

The owner of the Amorepacific Company is a great example of a client in search of high quality and good design. While the book only features the company's research and design centre, we designed additional buildings for the company's Yongin-Si campus. The client was particularly concerned with the well-being of their employees. More than a series of buildings, the main task was to create a peaceful and pleasant environment for all staff members.

Speaking of environment, a peculiar aspect of the Mimesis Museum project was indeed its lack of built context. In fact, Paju Book City was a newly planned city, and therefore the museum had no pre-existing architectural reference. On the other hand, due to its use as a cultural centre and museum, it was destined to be a reference unto itself. For this reason, it is an introspective building with few relations to its surroundings. The museum has been very well built, and both the concrete of the exterior and the plaster of the interior have been carefully crafted. I have a very good memory of this project because I was also allowed to control the interior design and finishings, something that is becoming increasingly rare in Europe and specifically in Portugal...

For the Saya Park Art Pavilion in Gyeongsangbuk-do, the client played even more of a central role than in the previously mentioned projects. Yoo Jae Sung – a wealthy steel entrepreneur – decided to build a pavilion that I had designed almost twenty years prior to house *Guernica* (1937) by Picasso. This was just a conceptual proposal I had been invited to draw in connection to the celebrations of Madrid Cultural Capital of Europe in 1992... It was not conceived to be actually built, in fact, we had to reduce its dimensions because the original project was huge. When he contacted me through Carlos Castanheira – the architect I used to work with on commissions in the Far East – I immediately underlined that the project was conceived to host two important Picasso works...What would he intend to exhibit there? He promptly answered with no uncertainty: 'You are also a sculptor, aren't you? So we will show your own sculptures!' This is quite funny because nobody in Portugal seems to be interested in my sculptural works...

DM: Coming back to Europe, you recently completed a church in Brittany, close to Rennes: the Anastasis Church. Twenty-five years have passed since the completion of the Santa María Church; what reminds you of that project in this new challenge?

AS: Again, an important commonality between the two projects is the commitment of the client. We have already talked about the important role of Don Higino in the construction of Marco de Canaveses church... A similar role was played in Saint-Jacques-de-la-Lande by the Archbishop of Rennes, Pierre d'Ornellas. A very intelligent man – of Portuguese origin, by the way – a true expert in liturgical matters. We had thoughtful conversations about the creation of sacred

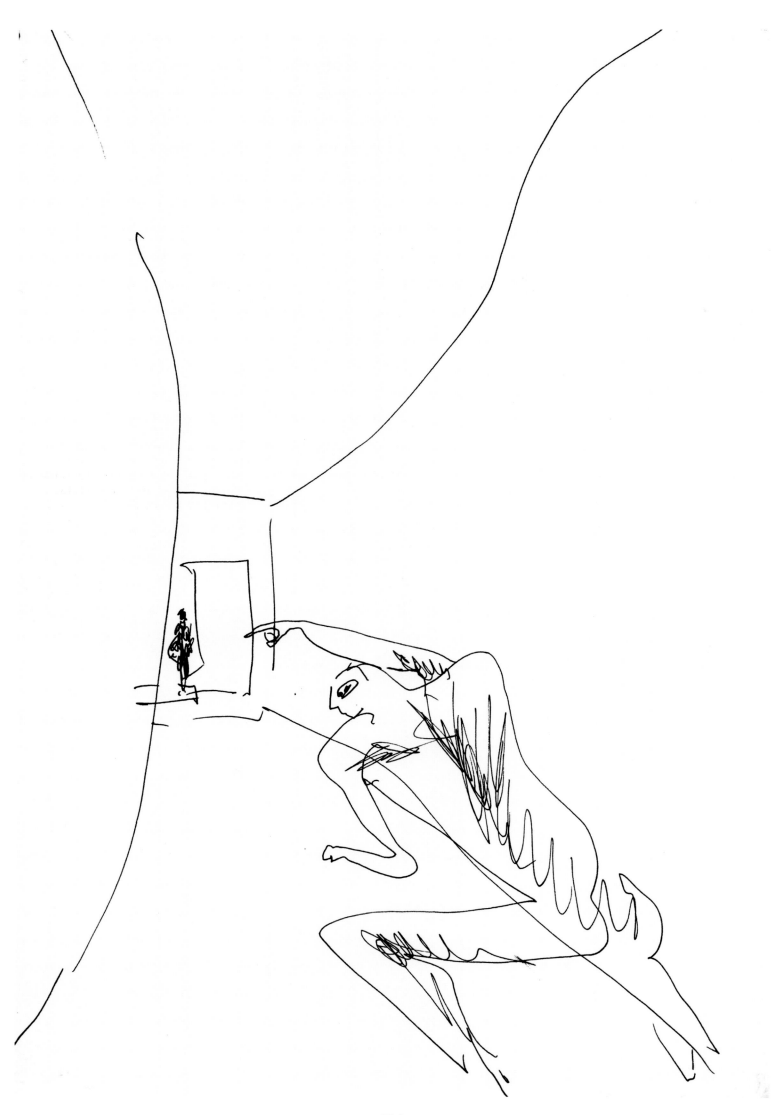

spaces, and it was a very enriching relationship, particularly because sometimes we would be in complete agreement, and other times held very different points of view. I really enjoyed this dialectic way of developing the project. One result of this exchange of ideas was the unusual decision to place the church on the first floor, implying a sense of ascension to the parishioner as well as providing more direct contact with the exterior of the parish centre.

The Leça da Palmeira Ocean Swimming Pools are a good example of the 'European' rhythm we were talking about, in comparison with the Korean effectiveness. The pools took five years to be completed despite it being a very easy project in principle. They started out as simple marine ponds, but soon the public health department demanded that we incorporate water treatment, then lavatories, then changing rooms. Later, the client wanted to add a bar. The programme was constantly evolving. I was young, and it was the only project I had in hand at the time, so I was spending whole days at the construction site. For me, it was a great experience because it came after the Casa de Chá Boa Nova project, and with the pools, I was somehow able to correct the relationship with nature that had not quite convinced me in the earlier project. Here, the relationship is much more marked: architecture is geometry, and nature is nature. The key lies in the well-defined encounter between these two worlds.

Over the years, this coastal facility has also experienced the lack of maintenance we were talking about earlier. In this case, I would say it is even worse, since the area has suffered real damage, having been left at the mercy of the various concessionaires, since no one from the city council controlled their actions. In fact, the recent refurbishment was a very difficult job because of the type of building it is; it is really difficult to intervene on exposed concrete. The main instruction I left at my first site visit regarding the quality of the new interventions, was: 'the worse the better!' This was in order to avoid a too blatant contrast between the pre-existing and the repaired parts.

DM: So, do we end up with a happy or unhappy project?

AS: Well, in this case I think that the construction defects are less relevant than in other projects, but the vandalism and lack of care that the complex endured made me suffer for many years. Nor does it help that, at the time, my plan for the adjacent coastal road, which the city council ignored for decades, was not taken into consideration. It was finally only partially executed not long ago, but unfortunately by then the surroundings had already been compromised by the speculative urbanisations previously carried out... In short, we end up with some unhappiness...

304   Sketch from the series 'Visions for Madrid'.

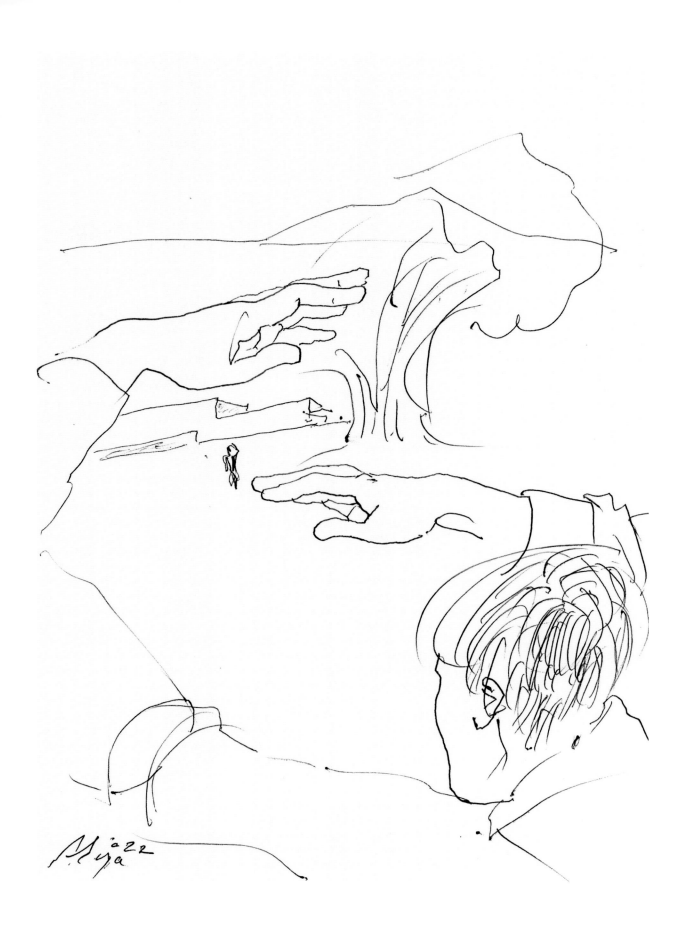

306   Architecture through Photography, a recent
sketch by Álvaro Siza conceived to close this book.
307   The first photograph Duccio Malagamba took
of a project by Álvaro Siza. The picture was taken by
Malagamba during a Summer trip to Portugal in 1984.

PROJECT LIST

OCEAN SWIMMING POOLS
Leça da Palmeira, Portugal
1961–1966
Collaborators
António Madureira
Beatriz Madureira
Francisco Guedes de Carvalho

SAAL BOUÇA SOCIAL HOUSING
Porto, Portugal
1972–2006
Collaborators
1st stage (1972–1978)
António Madureira
Francisco Guedes de Carvalho
Adalberto Dias
Miguel Guedes de Carvalho
Eduardo Souto de Moura
Maria Manuela Sambade
Nuno Ribeiro Lopes
José Paulo dos Santos
2nd stage (1999–2006)
Rosário Borges de Pinho
Raquel Paulino
João Cabeleira
Paulo Sousa
Ana Costa e Silva

COLLEGE OF EDUCATION
Setúbal, Portugal
1986–1994
Collaborators
José Paulo dos Santos
Jorge Nuno Monteiro
João Pedro Xavier
Anton Graf
Tiago Faria
Helena Torgo
Pascale de Weck

**GALICIAN CENTRE
OF CONTEMPORARY ART**
Santiago de Compostela, Spain
1988–1993
Principals in Charge
Concept design
Joan Falgueras
1st stage
Yves Stump
2nd stage
João Sabugueiro
Collaborators
Mona Trautman
Jane Considine
Tiago Faria
Anton Graf
Cecilia Lau
Elisiário Miranda
Luis Miguel Cardoso
Miguel Nery

**SANTA MARIA CHURCH
AND PARISH CENTRE**
Marco de Canaveses, Portugal
1990–2004
Rolando Torgo
Collaborators
Edite Rosa
Tiago Falcão
Miguel Nery
Rui Castro
Roger Lundeen
César Escudero

**SERRALVES MUSEUM
OF CONTEMPORARY ART**
Porto, Portugal
1991–1999
Principal in Charge
Clemente Menéres Semide
Collaborators
1st stage
Tiago Faria
2nd stage
Christian Gaenshirt
Sofia Thenaisie Coelho
3rd stage
Edison Okumura
Abílio Mourão
Avelino Silva
João Sabugueiro
Cristina Ferreirinha
Taichi Tomuro
Daniela Antonucci
Francesca Montalto
Francisco Reina Guedes
Ulrich Krauss

**FACULTY OF INFORMATION
SCIENCES**
Santiago de Compostela, Spain
1993–2000
Principals in Charge
Carlos Seoane
Marco Rampulla
Collaborators
Cristina Ferreirinha
Edison Okumura
Gonzalo Benavides
Javier Molina
Lia Kiladis
Luis Diaz-Mauriño

**INSEL HOMBROICH
ARCHITECTURE MUSEUM**
Neuss, Germany
1995–2008
Rudolf Finsterwalder

VMD HOUSE AND ART GALLERY
Oudenburg, Belgium
1997–2003
Collaborators
Roberto Cremascoli
Daniela Antonucci
Maurice Custers
Miguel Nery
Avelino Silva
Andrea Smaniotto
Ulrich Krauss
Christian Kieckens
Kristoffel Boghaert
Karen Van de Steene
Filip Verbeke

**ZAIDA BUILDING
AND COURTYARD HOUSE**
Granada, Spain
1998–2006
Principal in Charge
Hans Ola Boman
Site architect
Juan Domingo Santos
Collaborators
Luís Dias
Peter Testa
Francisco Silvestre Navarro
Edison Okumura
Emilio Horneros
Martin Hochrein

**IBERÊ CAMARGO
FOUNDATION MUSEUM**
Porto Alegre, Brazil
1998—2008
Principals in Charge
Barbara Rangel
Pedro Polónia
Collaborators
Michele Gigante
Francesca Montalto
Atsushi Ueno
Rita Amaral

**RIBERA SERRALLO
SPORTS COMPLEX**
Cornellà de Llobregat, Spain
2000—2006
Principals in Charge
1st stage
Marco Rampulla
2nd stage
José Manuel Pelegrin
Collaborators
Markus Elmiger
Gabriel Flórez
Atsushi Ueno
Pedro Polónia
Rita Amaral
Luis Fullola

MUNICIPAL LIBRARY
Viana do Castelo, Portugal
2001—2007
Principals in Charge
1st stage
Tatiana Berger
2nd stage
José Manuel Pelegrin
Collaborators
Edison Okumura
Maria Moita
Francisco Reina Guedes
Miguel Capllonch

FAMILY HOUSE
Sintra, Portugal
2002—2007
António Madureira
Collaborators
João Cabeleira
Rosário Borges de Pinho
Raquel Paulino
Paulo Sousa

SUMMER HOUSE
Majorca, Spain
2002—2008
Principals in Charge
1st stage
Atsushi Ueno
2nd stage
Hans Ola Boman
Site architects
Rafael Moranta
Miguel Capllonch

ADEGA MAYOR WINERY
Campo Maior, Portugal
2003—2006
Principal in Charge
Avelino Silva
Collaborator
Rita Amaral

MIMESIS MUSEUM
Paju Book City, South Korea
2006—2009
Carlos Castanheira
Jun Sung Kim
Principals in Charge
Dalila Gomes
Site architect
Young-il Park
Collaborators
Chungheon Han
João Figueiredo

**AMOREPACIFIC RESEARCH
AND DESIGN CENTRE**
Yongin-Si, South Korea
2007—2010
Carlos Castanheira
Kim Jong Kiu
Principals in Charge
Pedro Carvalho
Site architect
MARU
Collaborators
Eliana Sousa
Im Yo Jin
Ricardo Serra
Patricia Carvalho
João Figueiredo

ANASTASIS CHURCH
Saint-Jacques-de-la-Lande, France
2012—2018
Jean-Pierre Pranlas-Descours
Principal in Charge
Rita Amaral
Collaborators
Avelino Silva
Clemente Menéres Semide
Ana Silva
Cristina Ferreirinha
Louise de Chatellus
Delphine Bresson

SAYA PARK ART PAVILION
Gyeongsangbuk-do, South Korea
2015—2018
Carlos Castanheira
Collaborators
Rita Ferreira
Diana Vasconcelos
Luíza Felizardo
Nuno Rodrigues
Filipa Guedes

INDEX

Phaidon Press Limited
2 Cooperage Yard
London E15 2QR

Phaidon Press Inc.
111 Broadway
New York, NY 10006

phaidon.com

First published 2024

ISBN 978 1 83866 818 1

Commissioning Editor: Emilia Terragni
Project Editor: Stephanie Holstein
Book Concept and Design: Duccio Malagamba and Álvaro Siza
Production Controller: Lily Rodgers
Typesetting: Cantina

Printed in China

With special thanks to Beth Broome, Giovanna Borasi, Emma Caddy, Carlos
Castanheira, Alex Coco, Rosie Fairhead, Dani Gutiérrez, Anabela Monteiro,
Céline Pereira, Rosie Pickles, Maria João Pinto, Chiara Porcu, Jean-Pierre
Pranlas-Descours, and the owners of the properties featured.